C000066384

NEWMAN ON VATICAN II

Newman on Vatican II

IAN KER

OXFORD
UNIVERSITY PRESS

OXFORD
UNIVERSITY PRESS

Great Clarendon Street, Oxford, OX2 6DP,
United Kingdom

Oxford University Press is a department of the University of Oxford.
It furthers the University's objective of excellence in research, scholarship,
and education by publishing worldwide. Oxford is a registered trade mark of
Oxford University Press in the UK and in certain other countries

© Ian Ker 2014

The moral rights of the author have been asserted

First Edition published in 2014

All rights reserved. No part of this publication may be reproduced, stored in
a retrieval system, or transmitted, in any form or by any means, without the
prior permission in writing of Oxford University Press, or as expressly permitted
by law, by licence or under terms agreed with the appropriate reprographics
rights organization. Enquiries concerning reproduction outside the scope of the
above should be sent to the Rights Department, Oxford University Press, at the
address above

You must not circulate this work in any other form
and you must impose this same condition on any acquirer

Published in the United States of America by Oxford University Press
198 Madison Avenue, New York, NY 10016, United States of America

British Library Cataloguing in Publication Data
Data available

Library of Congress Control Number: 2014933424

ISBN 978-0-19-871752-2

Links to third party websites are provided by Oxford in good faith and
for information only. Oxford disclaims any responsibility for the materials
contained in any third party website referenced in this work.

*For Donal, Elizabeth, and Julie who urged me to write
another book*

Acknowledgements

I am very grateful to Tom Perridge, my editor at Oxford University Press, for encouraging the idea of this book and for help in changing my original title.

I warmly thank Don Briel, Brett Lockhart, James Reidy, and Edward Short, who read all or parts of the typescript, for their comments and encouragement.

Acknowledgements are due to the editors of *Logos* and to Peeters Press for permission to reprint with modifications two previously published pieces.

Contents

Abbreviations

References to Newman's works are usually to the uniform edition of 1868–81 (36 vols), which was published by Longmans, Green, and Co. of London until the stock was destroyed in the Second World War. References to the volumes in the uniform edition are distinguished from those to other editions by not having a date or place of publication in brackets after the title. All references to *Apologia pro vita Sua, The Idea of a University*, and *A Grammar of Assent* are to the Oxford critical editions.

Apo.	*Apologia pro Vita Sua*, ed. Martin J. Svaglic (Oxford: Clarendon Press, 1967)
Ari.	*The Arians of the Fourth Century*
Ath. i, ii	*Select Treatises of St. Athanasius*, 2 vols
AW	*John Henry Newman: Autobiographical Writings*, ed. Henry Tristram (London and New York: Sheed and Ward, 1956)
Call.	*Callista: A Tale of the Third Century*
Campaign	*My Campaign in Ireland, Part I* (Aberdeen: A. King & Co., 1896)
Cons.	*On Consulting the Faithful in Matters of Doctrine*, ed. John Coulson (London: Geoffrey Chapman, 1961)
CS	*Catholic Sermons of Cardinal Newman*, ed. at the Birmingham Oratory (London: Burns & Oates, 1957)
DA	*Discussions and Arguments on Various Subjects*
Dev.	*An Essay on the Development of Christian Doctrine*
Diff. i, ii	*Certain Difficulties Felt by Anglicans in Catholic Teaching*, 2 vols
Ess. i, ii	*Essays Critical and Historical*, 2 vols
GA	*An Essay in Aid of a Grammar of Assent*, ed. I.T. Ker (Oxford: Clarendon Press, 1985)
HS i, ii, iii	*Historical Sketches*, 3 vols
Idea	*The Idea of a University*, ed. I.T. Ker (Oxford: Clarendon Press, 1976)
Jfc.	*Lectures on the Doctrine of Justification*

LD	*The Letters and Diaries of John Henry Newman*, ed. Charles Stephen Dessain et al., vols i–x (Oxford : Clarendon Press, 1978–2006), xi–xxii (London : Thomas Nelson and Sons, 1961–72), xxiii–xxxii (Oxford: Clarendon Press, 1973–2008)
LG	*Loss and Gain: The Story of a Convert*
MD	*Meditations and Devotions of the Late Cardinal Newman* (London: Longmans, Green, and Co.,1893)
Mix.	*Discourses Addressed to Mixed Congregations*
Moz. i, ii	*Letters and Correspondence of John Henry Newman during his Life in the English Church*, ed. Anne Mozley, 2 vols (London: Longmans, Green, and Co., 1891)
NO	*Newman the Oratorian: His Unpublished Oratory Papers*, ed. Placid Murray, OSB (Dublin: Gill and Macmillan, 1969)
OS	*Sermons Preached on Various Occasions*
PS i–viii	*Parochial and Plain Sermons*, 8 vols
SD	*Sermons Bearing on Subjects of the Day*
SN	*Sermon Notes of John Henry Cardinal Newman, 1849–1878*, ed. Fathers of the Birmingham Oratory (London: Longmans, Green, and Co., 1913)
TT	*Tracts Theological and Ecclesiastical*
US	*Fifteen Sermons Preached before the University of Oxford*
VM i, ii	*The Via Media*, 2 vols
VV	*Verses on Various Occasions*

Introduction

Ever since the Second Vatican Council, it has become a commonplace to refer to John Henry Newman as 'the Father of Vatican II'. A century before the theological revival that came to be known as the *nouvelle théologie* began in France in the 1930s, a revival that paved the way for the teachings of the Council, Newman and his fellow Tractarians in the Oxford Movement were already seeking to return to the sources of Christianity in the writings of the Fathers. The leading French theologians who initiated the 1930s *ressourcement* movement, Yves Congar, Jean Daniélou, and Henri de Lubac, were concerned to escape from the desiccated neo-scholasticism that was the dominant theology then of the Roman Catholic Church, a theology which had lost touch not only with the Fathers but with St Thomas Aquinas himself. The Tractarians, on the other hand, were preoccupied with formulating a patristic theology that could form the basis of a Catholic revival in the Church of England. The first volume of the Tractarian *Library of the Fathers* was published in 1838, while Daniélou and de Lubac began the *Sources Chrétiennes* series just over a hundred years later in 1942.

In Newman, the leading Tractarian theologian, as well as 'perhaps the most seminal Roman Catholic theologian of modern times',[1] the theologians of the *nouvelle théologie* found not only a theologian whose theology was based on that of the Fathers, but a theologian who was clear that theology should not be separated from history, whose principal theological work indeed was on the development of doctrine, a theologian who emphasized the real and the concrete as opposed to the notional and abstract, the personal and the experiential as opposed to the impersonal and theoretical, and who believed that he was the first theologian to make '*life* the mark of a true Church'.[2] Newman's theology was indeed the antithesis of

---

[1] Avery Dulles, SJ, 'The Threefold Office in Newman's Ecclesiology', in Ian Ker and Alan G. Hill, eds, *Newman after a Hundred Years* (Oxford: Clarendon Press, 1990), 375.

[2] *LD* xi.101.

neo-scholasticism, a fact that caused him a great deal of tribulation during his Catholic life. This suffering also made him a highly sympathetic figure to the theologians of the *nouvelle théologie*, who also suffered at the hands of the Roman authorities in their attempt to renew Catholic theology by returning not only to the Scriptures and the Fathers but also to St Thomas Aquinas's writings themselves rather than the later sixteenth- and seventeenth-century commentaries on them, which neo-scholasticism regarded as authoritative.[3]

There is no doubt only one text in the documents of Vatican II where Newman's influence can be directly felt: in the Dogmatic Constitution on Divine Revelation, *Dei Verbum*, article 8, where the Council acknowledges the fact of doctrinal development. However, there are several other very important documents that Newman anticipated, particularly the Constitution on the Church (*Lumen Gentium*), the most important document of a Council which was principally concerned with the Church, and to which his writings offer a valuable and even corrective hermeneutic where the meaning of the conciliar texts has been exaggerated or distorted or neglected. With the imminent approach of the fiftieth anniversary of the end of the Council, this seems an opportune time to consider the teachings of the Council, as well as their subsequent interpretation, in the light of Newman's thought and writings.

Newman himself has very frequently suffered from selective quotation, without regard to the context and without taking into consideration what he says elsewhere on the subject in question. As Avery Dulles has rightly insisted, 'Newman cannot be studied through excerpts, but only by a grasp of his thinking in its full range.'[4] Thus one can quote Newman's forthright statement in the *Apologia* that dogma was 'the fundamental principle' of his religion ('I know no other religion'),[5] or his insistence in the speech he made on being made a cardinal that 'For thirty, forty, fifty years I have resisted to the best of my powers the spirit of liberalism in religion' (that 'great mischief')[6]—and conclude from these two quotations that Newman was an extremely conservative and traditionalist thinker.[7] Or again,

[3] For a historical account of the *nouvelle théologie* movement, see Jürgen Mettepenningen, *Nouvelle Théologie—New Theology: Inheritor of Modernism, Precursor of Vatican II* (London and New York: T & T Clark International, 2010).

[4] Avery Cardinal Dulles, SJ, *Newman* (London and New York: Continuum, 2002), 113.

[5] *Apo.* 54.   [6] *Campaign* 395.

[7] See, for example, Stanley L. Jaki, *Newman's Challenge* (Grand Rapids, MI: William B. Eerdmans, 2000).

on the other hand, one might quote Newman's famous words, 'I shall drink—to the Pope, if you please—still, to Conscience first, and to the Pope afterwards,'[8] or his apparently uncompromising words, 'Theology is the fundamental and regulating principle of the whole Church system'[9]—and conclude that Newman was a forerunner of the liberal, 'spirit of Vatican II' kind of theologian who justifies dissent from the Church's teachings and believes in a kind of parallel magisterium of the theologians.[10]

In the first chapter of this book I shall show how these apparently very different sentiments are not inconsistent or self-contradictory, but can be reconciled within the whole spectrum of Newman's thought. For the truth is that Newman was not *tout court* simply conservative or simply liberal, but nor on the other hand was he merely confused and muddled. Instead, he was a highly complex and subtle thinker who refused to see issues in black and white alternatives. He was both radical and conservative, a reformer but also a traditionalist. It is important to be clear about his nuanced theological stance before considering what he might have to say about the documents of Vatican II and the post-conciliar Church.

If Newman's theology is both innovative and conservative, his own theological development evinces both change and continuity. And it is, of course, the reconciliation of change with continuity that his theory of doctrinal development, which is the subject of the second chapter, attempts to address. Before applying the seven 'tests' or 'notes' that Newman suggests for distinguishing between authentic development (where there is both change and continuity) and corruption (where there is change without continuity) to his own theological development, I examine the various charges that have been brought against the accuracy (or even truthfulness) of the account he gives of his religious history in the *Apologia pro Vita Sua*. Newman's seven 'tests' or 'notes' have often been dismissed as practically useless, but I maintain that they show their relevance and usefulness when they are applied to the most controversial of the documents of Vatican II, the Declaration on Religious Freedom (*Dignitatis Humanae*), the document which most obviously raised the question of development or corruption: was this evident change in the Church's teaching a *volte*

---

[8] *Diff.* ii.261.   [9] *VM* i.xlvii.
[10] See, for example, John R. Connolly, *John Henry Newman: A View of Catholic Faith for the New Millennium* (Lanham, MD: Rowman & Littlefield, 2005).

face or could it be reconciled with the Church's tradition; that is, was there continuity as well as change?

Before, during, and after the First Vatican Council Newman adumbrated in his private letters what amounts to a mini-theology of Councils, and in Chapter 3 I look at how far this theology can throw light on the meaning and implications of the Second Vatican Council. Newman was particularly interested in the historical connexions between Councils and how one Council modifies by adding to what a previous Council taught, and in how Councils represent both change and continuity. He was well aware that Councils cause great confusion and controversy, not least because their teachings, which require careful interpretation, are liable to be exaggerated by opposing protagonists, and that they can have very serious unintended effects. He was also struck by the significance of what a Council does *not* say. I argue that the silence of Vatican II on the subject of evangelization, which has become the most important item on the Church's agenda in these more recent post-conciliar years, is an excellent example of this. And I suggest that the new so-called ecclesial movements and communities, which have grown rapidly since the Council, are not only a response to this silence, but are also a concrete realization of the organic ecclesiology of the first two chapters of the Constitution on the Church (*Lumen Gentium*). These two chapters, in my view the most important texts of the Council, have been regularly ignored or misinterpreted in the post-conciliar period, but their true significance has been revealed in the movements and communities, which illustrates Newman's point in his *Essay on the Development of Christian Doctrine* that religious ideas become clearer in the course of time.

The first two chapters of *Lumen Gentium* also refer to the so-called charismatic dimension of the Church, an important rediscovery that has also been largely ignored or misunderstood in the years after the Council, and in Chapter 4 I show how important this dimension was for both the Anglican and the Catholic Newman. As effectively the founder and leader of the Oxford Movement, which consisted of both clergy and laity, Newman would have had a very clear understanding of the significance of the new ecclesial movements, while his own understanding of the origin and development of the Oratory of St Philip Neri (which he brought to England) would have made him very sympathetic to the new ecclesial communities.

Chapter 5 considers some other important documents of Vatican II and how they have been distorted through exaggeration, and how

Newman's own anticipations of their teachings provide a corrective hermeneutic. Once again Newman is shown to be both the radical reformer as well as the traditional conservative.

Chapter 6 turns to the post-conciliar Church and the need for a 'new evangelization' of secular post-Christians, and asks whether Newman can offer any contribution to this relatively new problem. In fact, Newman anticipated the phenomenon of secularization in a late, little known sermon, and had actually in effect proposed the kind of evangelization that was needed two decades earlier in his novel *Callista*, which he regretted had been neglected in his own time and which today even many students of Newman have never read. But the required kind of apologetic approach that Newman dramatizes in the novel he had already explained in one of his best Anglican sermons. As an Anglican preacher, he had been preoccupied with making real to his hearers the figure of the Christ of the Gospels, the reading of one of which finally converts the post-pagan heroine of *Callista*, who would have found in her creator's Anglican sermons the kind of catechesis she would need before receiving the sacraments of initiation into the Church—that is, the kind of personalist catechesis that Newman would surely recommend for the 'new evangelization'.

1

The Conservative Radical

I

1

Elected in 1822 to a fellowship at Oriel College, Oxford, then the most academically prestigious of the colleges, John Henry Newman found himself a member of the famous senior common room, which was dominated by the so-called 'Noetics', who emphasized the importance of reason in theology, as opposed to the Evangelicals who emphasized Scripture and the high church party which stressed tradition. Under their and other influences, Newman gradually abandoned the Evangelicalism to which he had been introduced by a schoolmaster seven years earlier when he was fifteen. By the end of 1827, he admitted in the *Apologia*, he was 'drifting in the direction of the Liberalism of the day', when he was 'rudely awakened' from his 'dream...by two great blows—illness and bereavement'.[1]

But the Oriel senior common room was only the tip of a much larger iceberg. In March 1829 Newman identified the threat that the spread of education represented for Christianity:

We live in a novel era—one in which there is an advance towards universal education. Men have hitherto depended on others, and especially on the Clergy, for religious truth; now each man attempts to judge for himself. Now without meaning of course that Christianity is in itself opposed to free inquiry, still I think it *in fact* at the present time opposed to the particular form which that liberty of thought has now assumed. Christianity is of faith, modesty, lowliness, subordination; but the spirit at work against it is one of latitudinarianism, indifference,

---

[1] *Apo.* 25–6.

republicanism, and schism, a spirit which tends to overthrow doctrine, as if the fruit of bigotry, and discipline as if the instrument of priestcraft.[2]

Already, four years before the beginning of the Oxford Movement, Newman sees liberalism as the great enemy, and not the Evangelicalism that he was abandoning, as has been claimed in a recent revisionist study.[3]

The threat of political interference in the Church of England by a reforming Whig administration (which was to come into power in November 1830) raised questions about the urgent need for internal reforms. But Newman was hostile to any attempt to change the liturgy, particularly the damnatory clauses in the Athanasian Creed: 'if certain parts offend certain minds, is there not on the other hand an extreme danger of countenancing the false liberality of the age, which would fain have it believed that differences of *opinion* are of slight consequence.'[4] In June 1830 Newman resigned his membership of the Bible Society because it encouraged 'coming on *common ground* with Dissenters': 'I do believe IT MAKES CHURCHMEN LIBERALS…it makes them feel a wish to conciliate Dissenters at the expense of truth.' However, the Bible Society was only one manifestation of the 'tendency of the age…towards *liberalism.*' It was the Church which was 'the *legitimate* enforcement of Christian truth. The liberals know this—and are in every possible manner trying to break it up.'[5]

In March 1831 the new Whig government began passing the great Reform Act through parliament. A commission had already been set up to look into ecclesiastical abuses such as pluralism in the established Church. 'The vital question was how were we to keep the Church from being liberalized?'[6] Most English people, Newman thought, did not really 'believe in Christianity in any true meaning of the word. No, they are liberals, and in saying this, I conceive I am saying almost as bad of them as can be said of any man.'[7] As the threat to the Church grew, 'Oxford will want hot-headed men, and such I mean to be, and I am in my place,' exclaimed Newman. And in his place he was when the election to the newly founded Sanscrit chair took place in February 1832, and one of the two candidates, the one who, Newman admitted, was the 'best' Sanscrit scholar available, H.H. Wilson, might be, he suspected, 'a mere liberal, and consider

---

[2] *LD* ii.129–30. [3] See Chapter 2, section 2, p. 43–5. [4] *LD* ii.191.
[5] *LD* ii.264–5. [6] *Apo.* 39. [7] *LD* ii.317.

the Sanscrit-theology not far inferior to the Christian'. The other candidate, W.H. Mill, 'a strict Churchman', narrowly lost the election in March in spite of Newman's best efforts.[8]

<h2 style="text-align:center">2</h2>

The year before, Newman had accepted an invitation from the high church Hugh James Rose to contribute a history of Church Councils to a new library of theological works, of which Rose was co-editor. However, at the end of August 1831, he informed Rose that the Eastern Councils would need a volume to themselves and that he was now concerned with how to organize this first volume. Newman did not see his work as merely academic research, since in writing it he was 'resisting the innovations of the day'—in other words liberalism.[9]

In the end, the book turned out to be not a history of the Councils, or even of the Council of Nicaea, but of the Arian heresy. Unsurprisingly, Rose's co-editor, W.R. Lyall, thought it unsuitable for their theological library which was intended for general readers. Apart from not being the work that had been commissioned, it was too specialized and there were also theological objections in Lyall's view. Most serious was Newman's treatment of the early Church's *disciplina arcani* or 'practice of economy' which implied a concept of tradition that seemed to Lyall 'directly adverse to that which Protestant writers of our own church have contended for' and too 'favourable to the Romanist writers'. Lyall also objected to Newman's notion of 'the *Dispensation of Paganism*', which he knew was 'a very common view of the matter' in Clement of Alexandria but which he thought 'open to very grave objections'. And to speak of 'the Heathen poets' having been 'divinely illuminated' could 'cast a doubt upon the whole doctrine of inspiration'. Lyall was also uneasy about the way Newman spoke of 'the backwardness of the Fathers, to put forward the great and peculiar doctrines of the Gospel': 'If it were true that the Ante-Nicene fathers had not spoken strongly and openly and frequently about these doctrines, it would be difficult not to believe that they had not interpreted Scripture as we do—a supposition that would be almost fatal to the doctrines as it seems to me...'[10] Newman's *The Arians of the Fourth Century*, then, was by no means simply the work of a conservative high church

---

[8] *LD* iii.15–16, 27.   [9] *LD* iii.43.   [10] *LD* iii.105, 113.

Anglican like Lyall, even though, as we have seen, Newman regarded it as directed against the liberals. This was a radical work of theology. Newman was anti-liberal but he was no mere conservative.

3

In December 1832 Newman set out on a Mediterranean cruise with his friend and colleague at Oriel Richard Hurrell Froude and his father. Recalling his thoughts at the time, he was convinced that 'if Liberalism once got a footing' in the Church, it was 'sure' of 'victory'. On arriving at Algiers, Newman 'would not even look at the tricolour': the mere sight of the republican flag reminded him unpleasantly of 'the success of the Liberal cause'.[11] In March 1833 he learned of the 'very comprehensive' plan of the latitudinarian Thomas Arnold, a former member of the Oriel Noetic common room, for reforming the Church to avoid the threat of disestablishment posed by the Whig government, whereby all the denominations except the Quakers and Roman Catholics would hold their services in the Anglican parish church. This exclusion of Quakers and Catholics, as well as Jews, seemed 'illiberal', Newman commented sarcastically.[12]

In January 1834 a private inquiry about the *disciplina arcani* or 'reserve of the Primitive Church in inculcating the more sacred doctrines of our faith', about which Newman had written in the *Arians*, elicited a reply that would have more than confirmed Lyall's unease about Newman's treatment of tradition. This 'rule of secrecy', Newman wrote, 'existed rather as a feeling and a principle than as a rule in the early Church':

> This is the case with the greater part of the theological and ecclesiastical system, which is implicitly contained in the writings and acts of the Apostles, but was developed at various times according to circumstances. I should in a certain sense say this was true of the doctrine of the Trinity—and of the Incarnation...[13]

The conservative high church Lyall was clearly fully justified in his unease: Newman the radical theologian had already grasped the concept of the development of doctrine. Again in 1834, in one of the early *Tracts for the Times*, *Tract 40*, which takes the form of a dialogue between a *Clericus* and a *Laicus*, the layman asks the priest to respond

---

[11] *Apo.* 42. [12] *LD* iii.258, 298. [13] *LD* iv.179–80.

to objections that his 'religious system' ('the Apostolical'), in other words Tractarianism, is in fact 'Popery'. The priest, clearly Newman himself, maintains that 'fresh and fresh articles of faith are necessary to secure the Church's purity, according to the rise of successive heresies and errors. These articles were all hidden, as it were, in the Church's bosom from the first, and brought out into form according to the occasion.' When Newman republished the Tract in 1877, he added a footnote confirming that: 'Here...the principle of doctrinal development is accepted as true and necessary for the Christian Church.'[14]

The year before a similarly radical Newman had acknowledged 'a tendency', in the face of the Whig government's threat to the Church, 'which may grow, towards agitating for...the independence of Bishops of the Crown which has now become but a Creature of an Infidel Parliament...'[15] Although disestablishment would have serious financial consequences, he was not afraid of being, as he put it, 'thrown on the people'. However, he would not 'advocate a separation of Church and State, unless the Nation does more tyrannical things against us; but I do feel I should be glad if it were done and over, much as the Nation would lose by it—for I fear the Church is being corrupted by the union'. The fact was that, although he was still a Tory 'theoretically and historically', he was beginning 'to be a Radical practically'.[16]

In August 1834 Newman told Rose that R.D. Hampden, a former fellow of Oriel, who had been his successful rival for the chair of moral philosophy in March, had published a pamphlet in which 'he calls all articles impositions of human authority' and was advocating the abolition of subscription to the Thirty-Nine Articles as a condition for matriculation at Oxford. In November he wrote to Hampden himself to thank him for sending him a copy of his pamphlet and took the opportunity to express his 'very sincere and deep regret that it has been published'. A second edition of the pamphlet had appeared, in which the author wondered whether there was 'foundation for the common prejudice, which identifies systems of doctrine—or theological propositions methodically deduced and stated—with the simple religion of Jesus Christ, as received into the heart and influencing

---

[14] *VM* ii.40. See Chapter 2, section 2, p. 45–8 for attempts to deny that Newman had early on grasped the concept of doctrinal development and at least by 1834.
[15] *LD* iii.293.   [16] *LD* iv.34–5.

conduct'. Newman's response was that such an anti-dogmatic view tended 'altogether to make shipwreck of Christian faith'.[17] In February 1836 Hampden was appointed to the Regius Professorship of Divinity. Newman sat up all night working on a pamphlet, *Elucidations of Dr. Hampden's Theological Sentiments*, a copy of which he sent to Hampden, who, furious at the accusation that he had denied the Trinity and Incarnation were revealed doctrines, made a very significant distinction. 'It is one thing,' he replied, 'to speak of truths themselves and another to speak of *modes of statement*, or the *phraseology* in which the truths are expressed.'[18]

4

In the autumn of the previous year Newman had published as *Tract 73 On the Introduction of Rationalistic Principles into Religion* (later republished as 'On the Introduction of Rationalistic Principles into Revealed Religion'[19]). It was a Tract against the latitudinarian or liberal party, of which Hampden, who regarded Unitarians as Christians, was the most extreme example. Defining rationalism as an 'abuse' of reason, Newman wrote: 'To rationalize in matters of Revelation is to make our reason the standard and measure of the doctrines revealed.' But again Newman is no simple anti-liberal conservative, being careful to allow for a legitimate use of reason, which he contrasts with an illegitimate use:

> As regards Revealed Truth, it is not Rationalism to set about to ascertain, by the use of reason, what things are ascertainable by reason, and what are not; nor, in the absence of an express Revelation, to inquire into the truths of Religion, as they come to us by nature; nor to determine what proofs are necessary for the acceptance of a Revelation, if it be given; nor to reject a Revelation on the plea of insufficient proof; nor, after recognizing it as divine, to investigate the meaning of its declarations, and to interpret its language...This is not rationalism; but it is Rationalism to accept the Revelation, and then to explain it away; to speak of it as the Word of God, and to treat it as the word of man; to refuse to let it speak for itself; to claim to be told the *why* and the *how* of God's dealings with us...and to assign to Him a motive and a scope of our own; to stumble at the partial knowledge of what He may give us of them; to put aside what is obscure, as if it had not been said at all;

---

[17]   *LD* iv.323, 371.   [18]   *LD* v.235.   [19]   *Ess* i.30–48.

to accept one half of what has been told us, and not the other half; to assume that the contents of Revelation are also its proof; to frame some gratuitous hypothesis about them, and then to garble, gloss, and colour them, to trim, clip, pare away, and twist them, in order to bring them into conformity with the idea to which we have subjected them.

Theological liberalism led to the rejection of 'the idea of mystery'. But it was Newman's grasp of the mystery of Revelation that saved him from any kind of simplistic dogmatism. 'Considered as a Mystery,' Revelation, he insists, 'is a doctrine enunciated by inspiration, in human language, as the only possible medium of it, and suitably, according to the capacity of language; a doctrine *lying hid* in language, to be received in that language.' Dogmas are necessary, but they cannot fully comprehend the mystery, such are the limitations of language. 'A Revelation', Newman writes, 'is religious doctrine viewed on its illuminated side; a Mystery is the selfsame doctrine viewed on the side unilluminated. Thus Religious Truth is neither light nor darkness, but both together...Revelation...is not a revealed *system*, but consists of a number of detached and incomplete truths belonging to a vast system unrevealed, of doctrines and injunctions mysteriously connected together.'[20]

In the summer of 1838 Newman delivered twelve 'Lectures on the Scripture Proof of the Doctrines of the Church', of which eight were published as *Tract 85*, in which he declared that it was hard to take liberal Protestantism seriously: 'Why should God speak, unless He meant to say something? Why should He say it, unless He meant us to hear?' If there has been a revelation, then 'there must be some essential doctrine proposed by it to our faith'; and therefore it is difficult 'to be a consistent Latitudinarian', because even he will hold on to 'his own favourite doctrine, whatever it is'. It is against 'the common sense

---

[20] *Ess.* i.31–2, 41–2. Colin Gunton, 'Newman's Dialectic: Dogma and Reason in the Seventy-Third *Tract for the Times*', in Ian Ker and Alan G. Hill, eds, *Newman after a Hundred Years* (Oxford: Clarendon Press, 1990), 315–16, accuses Newman of evading here 'the need to be systematic', thus giving 'the impression of mystery mongering'. But this is to ignore what Newman says of the legitimate use of reason in theology. Gunton refers to Newman's treatment of the Trinity in the *Grammar of Assent*, claiming that he asserts that it is not possible 'to assent rationally' to the doctrine. But this is totally to misunderstand Newman's argument which is that it is possible to assent '*notionally*' and therefore rationally but not '*really*': 'the dogma of the Holy Trinity, as a complex whole, or as a mystery, is not the formal object of religious [i.e. 'real'] apprehension and assent; but as it is a number of propositions, taken one by one. That complex whole also is the object of assent, but it is the notional object...' (*GA* 88).

of mankind' to have 'a religion without doctrines': 'Religion cannot but be dogmatic; it ever has been.'[21] Two years later, he remarked that 'Latitudinarianism is an unnatural state; the mind cannot long rest in it; and especially if the fact of a revelation be granted, it is most extravagant and revolting to our reason to suppose that after all its message is not ascertainable and that the divine interposition reveals nothing.'[22]

5

In January 1841 Newman published a review article of the latitudinarian Henry Hart Milman's *History of Christianity*. Milman had already caused a stir with his *History of the Jews* in 1829. Newman's response then was again not that of a simple anti-liberal conservative. On the one hand, he thought the book 'very dangerous' and 'rationalistic'; on the other hand, 'the great evil' of the book lay, in his view, 'not in the *matter* of the history, but in the profane *spirit* in which it is written'— for in '*most* of his positions I agree with him but abhor the irreverent scoffing Gibbon-like tone of the composition'. The book was 'the fruit of a supercilious liberalistic spirit'.[23] As for this new book, while it was undoubtedly true that 'great portion of what is generally received as Christian truth, is in its rudiments or in its separate parts to be found in heathen philosophies and religions', Milman's conclusion did not follow that '"These things are in heathenism, therefore they are not Christian."' The right conclusion, rather, was that '"these things are in Christianity, therefore they are not heathen"':

> we prefer to say, and we think that Scripture bears us out in saying, that from the beginning the Moral Governor of the world has scattered the seeds of truth far and wide over its extent; that these have variously taken root, and grown up as in the wilderness, wild plants indeed but living; and hence that, as the inferior animals have tokens of an immaterial principle in them, yet have not souls, so the philosophies and religions of men have their life in certain true ideas, though they are not directly divine. What man is amid the brute creation, such is the Church among the schools of the world; and as Adam gave names to the animals about him, so has the Church from the first looked round upon the earth, noting and visiting the doctrines she found there...claiming to herself what they said rightly, correcting their errors, supplying

---

[21] *DA* 130–4.   [22] *LD* vii.412.   [23] *LD* ii.160, 299.

their defects, completing their beginnings, expanding their surmises, and thus gradually by means of them enlarging the range and refining the sense of her own teaching.

It was an eloquent development of what Newman had called in the *Arians* 'the *Dispensation of Paganism*',[24] namely the point that all religions have elements of the truth in them. This was very different from Milman's assumption that 'Revelation was a single, entire, solitary act...introducing a certain message' and that Christianity was 'some one tenet or certain principles given at one time in their fulness'. Rather, revealed religion was 'various, complex, progressive, and supplemental of itself'.[25] Newman's approach was certainly very different from the wholesale condemnation of Milman's book by conservative churchmen.

In *An Essay on the Development of Christian Doctrine*, published in 1845 immediately prior to his reception into the Roman Catholic Church, Newman quoted this passage from his review of Milman's book as the conclusion to his eighth chapter, 'Application of the Third Note of a True Development: Assimilative Power'.[26] Here, as in the review, he maintained that paganism and the heretical Christian 'sects...contained elements of truth amid their error'. But heresy was also beneficial to Christianity, as its 'doctrines...are indices and anticipations of the mind of the Church. As the first step in settling a question of doctrine is to raise and debate it, so heresies in every age may be taken as the measure of the existing state of thought in the Church, and of the movement of her theology; they determine in what way the current is setting, and the rate at which it flows.' The subsequent doctrinal definitions by the Church 'are the true fulfilment' of heretical 'self-willed and abortive attempts at precipitating the growth of the Church'. The Church is able 'by means of the continuity and firmness of her principles, to convert' the 'raw material' of heresy 'to her own uses. She alone has succeeded in thus rejecting evil without sacrificing the good...'. There was, Newman thought, 'a certain virtue or grace in the Gospel which changes the quality of doctrines, opinions, usages, actions, and personal characters when incorporated with it, and makes them right and acceptable to its Divine Author, whereas before they were either infected with evil, or at best but shadows of the truth'. Confident, then, 'in the power of

---

[24] *Ari.* 81.   [25] *Ess.* ii.231–3.   [26] *Dev.* 380–2.

Christianity to resist the infection of evil, and to transmute the very instruments and appendages of demon-worship to an evangelical use, and feeling also that these usages had originally come from primitive revelations and from the instinct of nature, though they had been corrupted; and that they must invent what they needed, if they did not use what they found; and that they were moreover possessed of the very archetypes, of which paganism attempted the shadows; the rulers of the Church from early times were prepared, should the occasion arise, to adopt, to imitate, or sanction the existing rites and customs of the populace, as well as the philosophy of the educated class'. And so the Church was able to 'convert heathen appointments into spiritual rites and usages'.[27] There was no question in Newman's mind of the falsity of paganism and heresy, no question that there was only one true religion and one true Church, but his response was not simply to condemn like the high church Lyall; it was a conservative yet radical response that anticipated the teaching of the Second Vatican Council.[28]

II

If Newman is best described theologically in his Anglican years as a conservative radical, what of Newman the Catholic?

1

Twelve years after his conversion to Rome, Newman wrote in a private letter that he was 'opposed to laymen writing Theology', not because they were laymen but because they were self-taught (the study of theology being then restricted to those training to become priests). Nor indeed did he 'exclude' himself although a priest: 'I have not written on dogmatics...since I have been a Catholic, and I suppose never shall—because I gave up private judgment when I became one.'[29] As a Catholic, he would not have thought of his Anglican theology as theology in the sense of what was then meant by Catholic theology—as

---

[27] *Dev.* 358, 362, 364–5, 379.   [28] See Chapter 5, section 5, p. 128–31.
[29] *LD* xvii.504.

he discovered when he arrived in Rome in 1846 to study for the priesthood only to discover that not even St Thomas Aquinas was studied,
let alone the Fathers upon whose writings his own Anglican theology
had been based.

However, as early as 1850 Newman had touched in a private letter
on an important ecclesiological issue that was eventually to cause him
much trouble with the Roman authorities. The re-establishment of a
Catholic hierarchy in September 1850 and a triumphalist pastoral letter by the newly created Cardinal Nicholas Wiseman led to a violent
campaign against the so-called 'Papal Aggression'. Faced with 'persecution', Newman thought that that it should be made an 'excuse... for
getting up a great organization, going round the towns giving lectures, or making speeches'. But such an initiative would inevitably be
predominantly lay, and would be quite unacceptable to the bishops.
Newman's own bishop had 'a terror of laymen', but Newman was convinced that the laity could 'be made in this day the strength of the
Church'.[30]

In 1851 Newman was invited to become the founding rector or
president of the new Catholic University of Ireland. The ostensible tar-
get of the *Discourses on the Scope and Nature of University Education*,
which were intended to launch the university and which were published in 1852, is the kind of liberal utilitarian criticism of a university
education within a confessional framework that had led to the founding of the secular University of London. Yet there is another less obvious and diametrically opposite point of view under more or less covert
attack—a conservative clerical Catholicism, which, Newman feared,
conceived of the new Catholic University of Ireland as a kind of glorified seminary rather than a proper university. Can the Pope, who has
recommended the establishment of the Catholic University, Newman
asks, have 'any obligation or duty at all towards secular knowledge
as such?... does he not contemplate such achievements of the intellect, as far as he contemplates, solely and simply in their relation to
the interests of Revealed Truth?' To the first question, Archbishop
Paul Cullen of Dublin, who had asked Newman to give the lectures
by way of advertising the new university, would surely have said 'no',
and to the second 'yes'. Newman seems to agree: 'if he encourages and
patronizes art and science, it is for the sake of Religion'. But the reason

<hr>

[30] *LD* xiv.214, 252.

that Newman attributes to the Pope is hardly the reason Cullen would have given: 'He rejoices in the widest and most philosophical systems of intellectual education, from an intimate conviction that Truth is his real ally, as it is his profession; and that Knowledge and Reason are sure ministers to Faith.' The Church 'fears no knowledge', for 'all branches of knowledge are connected together, because the subject-matter of knowledge is intimately united in itself, as being the acts and the work of the Creator.'[31] There is no opposition between faith and reason—both are to do with truth and 'truth cannot be contrary to truth'—and therefore no opposition between the Church and a proper university. However, Newman recognizes that faith and reason are not always in harmony: 'Right Reason, that is, Reason rightly exercised, leads the mind to the Catholic Faith, and plants it there, and teaches it in all its religious speculations to act under its guidance. But Reason, considered as a real agent in the world, and as an operative principle in man's nature... is far from taking so straight and satisfactory a direction.'[32]

Newman keeps both faith and reason, Church and university, in equipoise through the *Discourses*. Thus the eloquent 'imperial intellect', which is the goal of university education, is held in counterpoise with the authority of the Church. Or again, there is the contrast between the admission that a *Christian* literature is an impossibility, because it 'is a contradiction in terms to attempt a sinless literature of sinful man', and the insistence that nevertheless the study of literature must not be omitted from a Catholic university, because education is 'for this world' and 'it is not the way to learn to swim in troubled waters, never to have gone into them'. Conversely, the rapt evocation of the wonder of music is promptly followed by a warning against its temptation 'rather to use Religion than to minister to it'. Newman's advocacy of a liberal education is systematically qualified by reminders of its limitations: 'even what is supernatural need not be liberal... for the plain reason that one idea is not another idea':

> Its direct business is not to steel the soul against temptation...Quarry the granite rock with razors, or moor the vessel with a thread of silk; then you may hope with such keen and delicate instruments as human knowledge and human reason to contend against those giants, the passion and the pride of man.[33]

---

[31] *Idea* 6, 198, 94.   [32] *Idea* 372, 157.
[33] *Idea* 195, 197, 80, 101, 110–11.

However, the most remarkable and dramatic shift of perspective in the *Discourses* is to be found in the famous portrait of the so-called 'gentleman' in the eighth *Discourse*. Here Newman concludes his advocacy of a liberal education with an eloquent depiction of its 'momentous' moral effects 'all upon the type of Christianity...so much so, that a character more noble to look at, more beautiful, more winning, in the various relations of life and in personal duties, is hardly conceivable'. And yet 'the work is as certainly not supernatural as it is certainly noble and beautiful', for there is a 'radical difference' between this 'mental refinement' and 'genuine religion'. The Emperor Julian, 'in whom every Catholic sees the shadow of the future Antichrist', was 'all but the pattern-man of philosophical virtue'. Indeed, paradoxically, it is because of the very 'shallowness of philosophical Religion...that its disciples seem able to fulfil certain precepts of Christianity more readily and exactly than Christians themselves', so that 'the school of the world seems to send out living copies' of 'St. Paul's exemplar of the Christian in his external relations...with greater success than the Church'. Modesty is substituted for humility, and 'pride, under such training, instead of running to waste in the education of the mind, is turned to account'. A passage of wonderful irony follows, in which Newman admiringly extols the great and real social fruits of what he calls this 'self-respect'—only to conclude with devastating effect: 'It breathes upon the face of the community, and the hollow sepulchre is forthwith beautiful to look upon.' But the famous passage which follows, beginning with the well-known words, 'Hence it is that it is almost a definition of a gentleman to say that he is one who never inflicts pain', is so eloquent that it has often been assumed that this is Newman's ideal. And indeed it *is* Newman's ideal insofar as he sees such a person as the ideal product of a liberal education, which

> makes not the Christian, not the Catholic, but the gentleman. It is well to be a gentleman, it is well to have a cultivated intellect, a delicate taste, a candid, equitable, dispassionate mind, a noble and courteous bearing in the conduct of life;—these are the connatural qualities of a large knowledge; they are the objects of a University; I am advocating, I shall illustrate and insist upon them; but still, I repeat, they are no guarantee for sanctity or even for conscientiousness, they may attach to the man of the world, to the profligate, to the heartless...[34]

---

[34] *Idea* 129–30, 132–3, 164–5, 167, 174, 177–9, 110.

But if Newman is careful to insist on the limitations of a liberal education and the indispensable role of faith, it is worth noting what he has to say about the place of theology in the university. On the one hand, he makes it clear that the different branches of knowledge 'differ in importance', and that theology is the most important of all, for it 'comes from heaven' and 'does and must exercise' an 'important influence' over 'a great variety of sciences, completing and correcting them', for it is 'the highest indeed, and widest' of the branches of knowledge. But while theology is the most important branch of knowledge *qua* knowledge, it is not the most important subject for Newman educationally. He points out that in the middle ages the liberal arts were able to withstand the challenge presented by the new sciences of scholastic theology, law, and medicine, because they were 'acknowledged, as before, to be the best instruments of mental cultivation, and the best guarantees for intellectual progress'. For when it comes to education, 'the question is not what department of study contains the more wonderful facts...and which is in the higher and which in an inferior rank; but simply which out of all provides the most robust and invigorating discipline for the unformed mind'.[35]

On the question of the relation between theology and science, Newman on the one hand insists that the scientist 'should be free, independent, unshackled': reason should have nothing to fear from faith in a Catholic university. On the other hand, the scientist should take 'great care' to 'avoid scandal' by 'shocking the popular mind'. Still, he insists, there need be no conflict between science and theology which are 'two kinds of knowledge...separated off from each other; and cannot...contradict each other'.[36]

Finally, Newman was adamant that a Catholic university cannot be detached from the wider community of the Church. A Catholic university, he insisted, 'though it had ever so many theological Chairs, that would not suffice to make it a Catholic university; for theology would be included in its teaching only as a branch of knowledge'. Without the active presence of the Church, it would not be a real Catholic university: 'Hence a direct and active jurisdiction of the Church over it and in it is necessary, lest it should become the rival of the Church with the community at large in those theological matters which to the Church are exclusively committed,—acting as the

---

[35] *Idea* 54, 57–8, 92, 221–2.   [36] *Idea* 379, 381, 348.

representative of the intellect, as the Church is the representative of the religious principle.' As an example of how even the most apparently Catholic institution may be not authentically Catholic—but may actually be anti-Catholic—'without the direct presence of the Church', Newman takes the Spanish Inquisition, which 'was a purely Catholic establishment devoted to the maintenance, or rather the ascendancy of Catholicism, keenly zealous for theological truth, the stern foe of every anti-Catholic idea, and administered by Catholic theologians; yet it in no proper sense belonged to the Church. It was simply and entirely a State institution...it was an instrument of the State...in its warfare against the Holy See.' However ostensibly Catholic in its aims, 'its spirit and form were earthly and secular'. A Catholic university, therefore, Newman insists, cannot be properly Catholic 'without the Church's assistance; or, to use the theological term, the Church is necessary for its *integrity*'.[37]

The *Discourses*, which constitute the first half of *The Idea of a University*, still remain the great classic text on university education. But the Catholic University of Ireland has long ceased to exist. Newman himself resigned as president after only a few years in 1858 after a serious of frustrations at the hands of Archbishop Cullen in particular. In retrospect, Newman thought that the principal cause of the friction between himself and Cullen was his 'desire...to make the laity a substantive power in the University'. Thus he wanted the management of the finances to be in the hands of the laity who were paying for the university—but this was against all Irish clerical tradition, according to which the laity were to be 'treated like good little boys—were told to shut their eyes and open their mouths'. But, much worse from Cullen's point of view than Newman's abortive wish to have a lay finance committee, was his attitude to the 'young Ireland' or nationalist party, some of whose leading members were appointed to posts in the university in the face of strong opposition from Cullen, who had bitter memories of what Italian nationalists had done to the Church in Rome. Newman wanted all but the theology chairs to be filled by the ablest laymen (whatever their politics) rather than by academically inferior priests. Another initiative of Newman, to draw up a 'list of honorary members of the university, principally laymen from Ireland and elsewhere', was also viewed with suspicion by Cullen.[38]

---

[37] *Idea* 184–5.   [38] AW 326–8.

2

The question of the laity in the Church was now to emerge again in a different and much more serious context. In January 1857 Newman had written to J.M. Capes, the founder and editor of the liberal Catholic *Rambler* magazine, to say that he disapproved of what he considered to be an unorthodox article on original sin by Richard Simpson, the literary critic and Shakespearean scholar. But the reason for his writing was not primarily to criticize Simpson's article, but to commiserate with Capes over an attack by Cardinal Wiseman in the *Dublin Review* on the *Rambler* for causing dissension by advocating an improvement of Catholic educational standards. Once again Newman stood between conservative and liberal protagonists, approving and yet disapproving of the *Rambler*.

At the end of December 1858 Sir John Acton, the future Lord Acton, who had become the chief proprietor of the *Rambler*, came to see Newman about a letter that Simpson, who had replaced Capes as editor, had received from Wiseman, complaining about an article in the December issue by Johann Joseph Ignaz von Döllinger, the liberal Catholic German church historian, and threatening denunciation to Rome. Newman himself had already written to Acton to say that he was 'exceedingly interested' by the article, 'The Paternity of Jansenism', which its author attributed to St Augustine. Acton described their three-hour talk to Simpson and how Newman 'came out at last with his real sentiments to an extent which startled me...I did not think he could ever cast aside his diplomacy...so entirely, and was quite surprised at the intense interest he betrayed in the Rambler. He was quite miserable when I told him the news and moaned for a long time...'. But if Acton supposed that Newman was entirely on the side of the *Rambler*, he was mistaken. Although Newman could not see how Rome could condemn taking a 'historical view of the person of heretics, while condemning their writings', he could not helping thinking that 'the Rambler was in a false position', in so far as untrained laymen were writing about theology in a non-theological magazine and attacking authority as well. In conversation with Acton, he had admitted that authority could be misused, but now he warned that the 'position of the Holy See must be considered, especially in a missionary country', where it 'has to act, to act promptly and forcibly'.[39]

---

[39] LD xviii.525, 559 n. 3, 559–60.

Newman urged avoidance of theological controversy. Acton agreed, but doubted if it would be possible to discuss history or politics without provoking those whose bigotry opposed all free inquiry.

In January 1859 Newman wrote to tell Acton 'how much' he liked his article in the January issue on the kind of individual liberty which the Catholic doctrine of conscience demanded, a freedom which was better observed in Protestant England than in some Catholic countries.[40] This was to express a daringly radical view in a century when the very concept of religious freedom was being condemned by the papacy in Catholic countries where Catholicism was the official or established religion and where error was assumed not to have any rights—regardless of the people in error.[41] However, Newman was alarmed by another 'very startling article' by a leading inspector of schools, implicitly criticizing the bishops for their refusal to co-operate with a royal commission on primary education: Catholic schools received substantial financial support from the state and they should not resent an inquiry, even if it involved investigation into the way religion was taught. Towards the end of the month, Newman wrote again to warn Acton that he had heard definitely that the *Rambler* was to be 'denounced at Rome on several grounds' apart from the Döllinger article. In the event, Newman was asked by Bishop Ullathorne of Birmingham to mediate and to secure Simpson's resignation as editor. For his part, Newman told Simpson that he was 'exceedingly' pained at 'the very idea of the Rambler, which has done so much for us...being censured from authority'. Simpson wanted Newman to take over as editor. Although Newman only agreed for the moment to look over the proofs of the next issue, his fateful association with the *Rambler* had begun. He suggested a special section for letters, where controversial material could be deposited more safely. He agreed with Simpson that the bishops showed scant regard for the rights of the laity. In the end, the only person who was acceptable as editor to both Acton and Simpson and the bishops was Newman. Feeling it as a matter of conscience to do everything possible to keep in print a publication whose '*principles*' he was as anxious to further as he was to moderate its offensive '*tone*', Newman agreed to take over as editor. The 'animating principle' of the magazine, he reaffirmed in

---

[40] *LD* xix.17.
[41] For a discussion of this teaching and the Second Vatican Council's Declaration on Religious Freedom, see Chapter 2, section 4, p. 65–71.

the May number, was 'the refinement, enlargement, and elevation of the intellect in the educated classes'. He intended, he announced, 'to combine devotion to the Church with discrimination and candour in the treatment of her opponents; to reconcile freedom of thought with implicit faith; to discountenance what is untenable and unreal, without forgetting... the reverence rightly claimed for what is sacred; and to encourage a manly investigation of subjects of public interest under a deep sense of the prerogatives of ecclesiastical authority'. Warning was given that neither devotional nor theological works would be reviewed. Newman was well aware, of course, that he was caught 'between two fires'.[42]

When the May issue came out, Newman received a letter from a Father John Gillow, a professor of theology at Ushaw College, then the leading seminary in England, enclosing a pamphlet attacking the Döllinger article, and protesting against remarks about the bishops' recent pastoral letters on the royal commission on education. Newman acknowledged that the 'objectionable' passage had been written by himself, in which, while apologizing for any offence that had inadvertently been given to the bishops, he had stated boldly that the hierarchy should

> really desire to know the opinion of the laity on subjects in which the laity are especially concerned. If even in the preparation of a dogmatic definition the faithful are consulted, as lately in the instance of the Immaculate Conception, it is at least as natural to anticipate such an act of kind feeling and sympathy in great practical questions...

And he had warned against 'the misery of any division between the rulers of the Church and the educated laity'. He explained to Bishop Ullathorne that in his reference to the definition of the doctrine of the Immaculate Conception he had only been pointing out that 'the Christian people at large were consulted on the *fact* of the *tradition* of the Immaculate Conception in every part of the Catholic world'. He also explained to Gillow the sense in which he had used the word 'consult':

> To the unlearned reader the idea conveyed by 'consulting' is not necessarily that of asking an opinion. For instance, we speak of consulting a barometer about the weather. The barometer does not give us its

opinion, but ascertains for us a fact…I had not a dream of understanding the word…in the sense of *asking an opinion*.[43]

It is unfortunate that Newman did not foresee this misunderstanding which has persisted and given rise to the idea that he had said that the magisterium can only teach after asking the opinion of the laity. Bishop Ullathorne regretted that there seemed to be 'remains of the old spirit' in the *Rambler*: 'It was irritating. Our laity were a *peaceable* set.' Newman responded that he knew from experience that the laity in Ireland, for example, was 'unsettled'. In return, the Bishop wondered, 'Who are the laity?' Newman's answer was that 'the Church would look foolish without them'.[44] And so in the last number of the *Rambler* that he edited, Newman decided to deal more fully with the place of the laity in the Church.

'On Consulting the Faithful in Matters of Doctrine' was republished in 1961, just over a hundred years later on the eve of the opening of the Second Vatican Council. In his introduction, the editor, John Coulson, takes it for granted that the faithful are synonymous with the laity: 'not only is the existence of a lively and educated laity fundamental to his conception of the Catholic Church and to his theology, but…the most fruitful approach to his work is to see it as a developed theology of the laity in all its ramifications'. Coulson alternates between the words 'faithful' and 'laity' as though they were the same. Nor does he distinguish the bishops, with whom the article is concerned, from the clergy, as when he speaks of Newman's asking 'for the fullness of the Church to be made manifest, for that fullness which is not in the priests alone, but only in the conspiratio of priests and faithful laity'.[45] In his *Newman and the Common Tradition: A Study in the Language of Church and Society*, where he reproduces the substance of this introduction, Coulson sees Newman as protesting against the Church's being 'conceived as divided into two casts—the clerical or dynamic element; and the lay or passive element'.[46] Coulson's emphasis is on the words 'dynamic' and 'passive'—but the question is whether in fact Newman did conceive of the Church as fundamentally divided into the clerical and lay 'casts'.

The truth is that Newman equivocates in the sense that sometimes he speaks in scriptural and patristic terms and sometimes in

---

[43] *LD* xix.130–1, 135.   [44] *LD* xix.140–1.   [45] *Cons.* 20, 34.

[46] John Coulson, *Newman and the Common Tradition: A Study in the Language of Church and Society* (Oxford: Clarendon Press, 1970), 129.

the language of a later clericalized Church, that is, a Church that is seen as primarily divided into clergy and laity. From his study of the Greek Fathers Newman had learned that the Church is primarily the communion of those who have received the gift of the Holy Spirit in baptism, but he was living in the Tridentine Church of the nineteenth century, a Church that was conceived of as divided into the teaching (*docens*) and taught (*docta*) Church, a Church in which 'the "faithful" do not include the "pastors"'. Newman is quoting here the leading Roman theologian of the day, Giovanni Perrone, in order to point out that even Perrone acknowledges that the laity possess the *sensus fidelium* which witnesses to the Apostolic tradition. And Newman quotes Pope Pius IX in his bull of 1854 defining the doctrine of the Immaculate Conception, in which the Pope refers to the belief of the 'faithful' as one of the 'witnesses to the apostolicity of the doctrine': 'the two, the Church teaching and the Church taught, are put together, as one twofold testimony, illustrating each other, and never to be divided'.[47]

To prove that 'the voice of tradition may…express itself, not by Councils, nor Fathers, nor Bishops, but the "communis fidelium sensus"', Newman turns to that period of the Church which he knew so well, the fourth century. And he proceeds to argue that 'the Nicene dogma was maintained during the greater part of the 4th century…not by the unswerving firmness of the Holy See, Councils, or Bishops, but…by the "consensus fidelium"'.

> It is not a little remarkable, that, though, historically speaking, the fourth century is the age of doctors, illustrated, as it was, by the saints Athanasius, Hilary, the two Gregories, Basil, Chrysostom, Ambrose, Jerome, and Augustine, and all of these saints bishops also, except one, nevertheless in that very day the divine tradition committed to the infallible Church was proclaimed and maintained far more by the faithful than by the Episcopate.

In the passage of explanation that follows, it is noteworthy that Newman does not put the faithful laity on the one side and the unfaithful clergy on the other. On the contrary, 'there were numbers of clergy who stood by the laity and acted as their centres and guides'. Newman does not represent the clergy but the bishops as failing to uphold the orthodox doctrine: 'in that time of immense confusion the divine

---

[47] *Cons.* 65, 71.

dogma of our Lord's divinity was proclaimed, enforced, maintained, and (humanly speaking) preserved far more by the "Ecclesia docta" than by the "Ecclesia docens;" that the body of the episcopate was unfaithful to its commission, while the body of the laity was faithful to its baptism'. Later in the article, when Newman sets out his historical evidence, we learn that in Nicopolis *'there was a remarkable unanimity of clergy and people in rejecting'* the Arian bishop. The second point that is very striking is Newman's use of the word 'laity'. The very first of the texts he cites as 'proofs of the fidelity of the laity' speaks about the Arian bishops physically attacking the *'holy virgins and brethren'*, those who would now be called 'religious' and who are not classed among the laity.[48] Later in the same text of Athanasius the word *'virgins'* is again italicized to indicate that this is evidence for 'the fidelity of the laity'. Again, in the third of Newman's examples of the laity's fidelity, *'monasteries'* and *'monks'* are similarly italicized. In the fifth proof text, 'Flavian and Diodorus, who had embraced the ascetical life', or in other words were monks, are explicitly classed 'in the ranks of the laity', since 'they were not as yet in the sacred ministry'. Finally, when Newman came to republish *The Arians of the Fourth Century* in the uniform edition of his works, he added a note in the appendix, in which he republished part of the 1859 article with some amendments and some additions, including this sentence which begins with the remarkable words: 'in speaking of the laity, I speak inclusively of their parish-priests…at least in many places; but we are obliged to say that the governing body of the Church came short'. This sentence makes two things abundantly clear: first, that when Newman uses the word laity he is really speaking of the faithful, that is, those who are full of faith, whether they be lay people, religious or priests; second, that it is the failure of the bishops not the clergy with which the article is concerned. The idea that 'On Consulting the Faithful in Matters of Doctrine' is a kind of tract vindicating the rights of the laity in a clericalized Church is simply not supported by the text. It is true, of course, that the article arose out of the English bishops' refusal to consult with the laity about the royal commission on primary education.

---

[48]　According to *Lumen Gentium*, art. 43, religious life is 'not…a kind of middle way between the clerical and lay conditions', but rather 'a form of life to which some Christians, both clerical and lay, are called'. All quotations from Vatican II documents are taken from Austin Flannery, OP, ed., *Vatican Council II: The Conciliar and Post-conciliar Documents* (Dublin: Dominican Publications, 1975).

But once Newman steps back into the world of the fourth century, long before clericalization had produced the concept of a Church divided into clergy and laity, he is back in the kind of Church that St Paul describes in his letter to the Corinthians: 'Now you together are Christ's body; but each of you is a different part of it. In the Church, God has given the first place to apostles, the second to prophets, the third to teachers; after them, miracles, and after them the gift of healing; helpers, good leaders, those with many languages' (1 Cor. 12:27–8).

Since the Second Vatican Council, Newman has been regularly cited by liberal Catholics as a champion of what amounts to the 'laicization', as opposed to clericalization, of the Church; but the text of the 1859 article, the title of which is not 'On Consulting the Laity' but 'On Consulting the Faithful', shows that Newman's ecclesiology is a great deal more radical than that nineteenth-century ecclesiology, which ironically is shared by modern liberal Catholics, that defines the Church in terms of clergy and laity. It is a radical ecclesiology because it is rooted in the sources of the tradition, in the New Testament and the Fathers. We shall return to the article in Chapter 5 when we compare Newman's theology of the Church with that of the Second Vatican Council.

At the end of August 1859 Newman heard again from Gillow, who complained that the article appeared to be inconsistent with the doctrine of the infallibility of the Church. Newman responded that when he had spoken of 'a temporary suspense of the functions of the "Ecclesia docens"'[49], he had not meant 'failure' but something 'lighter even than "suspension"'. At the beginning of October, Bishop Brown of Newport delated the article to Rome. In the new year Newman wrote to Wiseman, who was in Rome, to ask what dogmas the offending article was supposed to have contravened and to say that he was ready to show that the article was fully consistent with them. The Congregation of Propaganda sent Wiseman a list of the objectionable passages, but this was never forwarded to Newman, with the result that he remained for years under a cloud at Rome. Newman, on the other hand, assumed the matter was closed when he heard nothing further. Ever since becoming a Catholic, he had intended to avoid the dangerous subject of theology; in the article he had been merely 'stating historical facts' which he assumed 'no one would deny'.[50]

[49] *Cons.* 77.   [50] *LD* xix.206, 420.

3

In June 1861 the crisis over the pope's temporal power, which was threatened by Garibaldi's invasion of the Papal States, threatened to drag Newman into another dangerous controversy. The general Catholic assumption then was that the pope's spiritual authority would be in danger if he ceased to be a temporal sovereign. Newman, however, thought that not only would the pope's 'real power' not be affected, but that when 'matters are finally settled, he will be stronger and firmer than he has been for a long while'—'Nothing is more wonderful in the past history of the Holy See than the transformation of its circumstances, and its power of beginning, as it were, a new life in them.' And, in fact, history showed that popes could be spiritually independent even when dependent on or even subject to an external political power; there was no reason why this should not be just as true if Rome were to become a neutral city. Nevertheless Newman refused an appeal from Acton to speak out in public. He agreed that it was 'very hard' that the *Rambler*, which had come out in support of the British government's opposition to the temporal power of the papacy, should not speak out on 'a point of ecclesiastical expediency'. But nevertheless to oppose 'legitimate authority' would put the *Rambler* in 'a false position'—'If they do not allow the Rambler to speak against the temporal power, they seem to me tyrannical—but they have the right to disallow it...'.[51] As before, Newman found himself caught between Acton and Simpson on the one hand and the bishops on the other hand, radical in his view of the temporal power, but conservative in his respect for authority.

In February 1864 Newman was very concerned at the 'fearfully important' news that the French liberal Catholic Count de Montalembert was threatened with condemnation for advocating religious freedom. The standard Catholic view then was that, since Catholicism was the true religion, both Church and state had the right to persecute heresy. But even if this was defensible in theory, this did not alter the practical fact that 'persecution does not answer...the feelings of the age are strongly against it as they were once for it. The age is such, that we must go by reason, not by force.' Indeed, Newman wondered if the presence of heresy was not actually beneficial, for 'the presence of Protestantism, where it is tolerated, stirs up Catholics and

<hr />

[51] *LD* xix.308–9, 506, 523.

keeps them from sinking...into tyranny, superstition, and immorality'. Admitting that religion could be established by the state if (and only if) this was the will of the people, even so, Newman argued,

> I am not at all sure that it would not be better for the Catholic religion every where, if it had no very different status from that which it has in England. There is so much corruption, so much deadness, so much hypocrisy, so much infidelity, when a dogmatic faith is imposed on a nation by law, that I like freedom better. I think Italy will be more religious, that is, there will be more true religion in it, when the Church has to fight for its supremacy, than when that supremacy depends on the provisions of courts, and police, and territorial claims.

It was true that 'it is the tendency of Christianity to impress itself on the face of society', but then it is also 'the tendency of devotion to increase Church lands and property', which led to corruption. The establishment of religion tended to lead not only to hypocrisy but also to state interference in the Church. And was there any 'proof that the Church saves *more* souls when established, than when persecuted, or than when tolerated?' Establishment was only justifiable anyway when '*Catholicism comes first and establishment comes second*', and when 'establishment is the spontaneous act of the people' and not of the Church; in such cases it was 'the will of the masses'; but it was 'not necessary for Catholicism'. Nor was it necessarily preferable: 'Is God glorified more by many saved or by great saints?' Such thoughts were, of course, extremely radical for a Catholic then to express:

> But we see every where a new state of things coming in, and it is pleasant to believe one has reasons not to fear it, but to be hopeful about it, as regards the prospects of religion. It is pleasant not to be obliged to resist a movement, which is so characteristic of the age; and with these feelings one may concur with Protestants in no small measure...

For one who had spent so much of his life fighting against the spirit of the age, it was a welcome development to be able to support this particular instance of 'progress'—not that he would be able to express publicly his support for Montalembert.[52] However, if Rome was foolish enough to condemn Montalembert, the condemnation would be of the theory of religious freedom, and it would still be open to a

---

[52]   *LD* xix.421, 432, 473; xx.477; xxi.41, 43.

Catholic politician to advocate toleration as the most practical policy in particular circumstances.

4

During April, May, and June 1864 Newman published in eight pamphlets his *Apologia pro Vita Sua*, in the last chapter of which he adumbrated a theology of authority and freedom in the Church. On the one hand, he was confronted with liberal Catholics like Acton and Simpson demanding theological freedom, and, on the other hand, by his Ultramontane fellow Oxford converts, the future Cardinal Manning, who was to be one of the principal advocates of the definition of papal infallibility in 1870, and W.G. Ward, who had recently published a pamphlet condemning religious freedom. Newman's response was that both freedom and authority are necessary, and that paradoxically a vibrant theology requires the boundaries and limitations of authority; the tension between authority and freedom is potentially creative rather than stultifying. Thus he is uncompromisingly insistent that the Church's infallibility is intended 'to restrain that freedom of thought, which of course in its self is one of the greatest of our natural gifts, and to rescue it from its own suicidal excesses'. And, although infallibility only pertains strictly to solemn dogmatic definitions, nevertheless Newman calls for respect for 'those other decisions of the Holy See, theological or not…which…come to me with a claim to be accepted and obeyed'. To the objection that, if so, then 'the restless intellect of our common humanity is utterly weighed down…so that…it is brought into order only to be destroyed'— Newman's response is that, on the contrary, the 'energy of the human intellect…thrives and is joyous, with a tough elastic strength, under the terrible blows of the divinely-fashioned weapon, and is never so much itself as when it has lately been overthrown'. Newman is not talking about a dialogue between theology and authority but a creative conflict: 'it is the vast Catholic body itself, and it only, which affords an arena for both combatants in that awful, never-dying duel'. After all, the Church can only define infallibly as a result of the work of theologians, of 'an intense and varied operation of the Reason, both as its ally, and provokes again, when it has done its work, a re-action of Reason against it', as theologians set to work to interpret the meaning of a definition and to determine its scope. Infallibility does not mean that 'the parties who are in possession of it are in all their proceedings infallible'—'history supplies us with instances in the Church, where legitimate power has been harshly used'. Nevertheless, Newman is quick to add, it does not 'follow that the substance of the acts of the ruling power is not right and expedient, because its manner may have been faulty'. Indeed, authority has been 'mainly in the right'. And this is true even when theology proposes what will eventually become a truth accepted by the Church. For his reading of Church history as an Anglican had shown Newman that 'the initial error of what afterwards became heresy was the urging forward some truth against the prohibition of authority at an unseasonable time'. The proof that infallibility has not stifled intellectual freedom in the Church is that it is 'individuals, and not the Holy See, that have taken the initiative, and given the lead to the Catholic mind, in theological inquiry'. Indeed, 'it is one of the reproaches against the Roman Church, that it has originated nothing, and has only served as a sort of…break in the development of doctrine'. Even Ecumenical Councils were guided by the 'individual reason' of theologians. Newman points out that paradoxically there 'never was a time when the intellect of the educated class was more active, or rather more restless than in the middle ages'. History showed how slow authority was in 'interfering' and how it was only after discussion and controversy among theologians and judgement by a bishop that a matter would come before the Holy See, only after it had been 'ventilated and turned over and over again, and viewed on every side of it' that 'authority is called upon to pronounce a decision, which has already been arrived at by reason'. However, Newman himself, of course, was living in an Ultramontane Church in which Rome was 'watching every word' uttered by a theologian, and theological freedom had indeed been crushed, as he implies in this imaginary (but very real) scenario. Still, he admits it is true that 'when controversies run high', then 'an interposition may…advisably take place; and again, questions may be of that urgent nature, that an appeal must…be made at once to the highest authority in the Church'.[53]

5

In September 1864 Rome condemned the Association for the Promotion of the Unity of Christendom. Although Newman thought

---

[53] *Apo.* 220, 225–6, 230–2, 237–9.

its members had been 'cruelly treated',[54] he had not felt able to join when it was founded in London seven years earlier. Newman had told its founder, the convert Ambrose Lisle Phillipps, that he could not accept that the Church of England enjoyed as an ecclesiastical body a 'religious existence'. However, even if he could not recognize the Church of England as a Church, he was not 'one of those who wish the Church Establishment of England overthrown'. Nor was he against ecumenical discussions, provided that people who ought to be Catholics did not attempt 'to *bargain* and make terms'. But he recognized that a certain 'economy' was necessary in dealing with Anglo-Catholics: 'they cling to points which never can be granted, but to tell them so' might 'throw them back'.[55]

Opposed as he was to the brutal suppression of the Association for the Promotion of the Unity of Christendom, he could not, like the liberal Phillipps, see 'the true fire' of Catholicism 'glimmering amid the ashes' of Anglicanism. Still, even if he could not pretend that Anglicanism was anything 'else than a tomb of what once was living, the casket of a treasure which has been lost', he was radical enough in his ecumenical theology to state that 'all other truths and acts of religion are included' in mere repentance and faith in Christ. He was sure that eventually there would be a reaction against Catholic bigotry, but he was less convinced that the Church of England would not become so 'radically liberalized... as to become a simple enemy of the Truth'.[56] As for corporate reunion of Canterbury with Rome, he thought it would be 'a miracle': 'To make that actual, visible, tangible body Catholic, would be simply to make a new creature—it would be to turn a panther into a hind'. Years before he had said that Anglicanism and Catholicism were two different religions proceeding on 'different *ideas*', so that whatever they might appear to have in common, 'yet the way in which those doctrines are held, and the whole internal structure in the two religions is different'. Nor was it at all inevitable that Anglo-Catholicism would continue to spread through the Church of England—it was more likely that there would be a reaction from the growing liberal wing. In addition, there were the Evangelicals to contend with, as well as 'the Erastian party, which embraces all three, and

[54] *LD* xxi.415.   [55] *LD* xviii.12, 71, 78, 100.
[56] *LD* xx.71, 172; xxi.249, 299.

against which there is no re-action at present, which *ever* has been, which is the *foundation* of Anglicanism.'[57]

The First Vatican Council opened on 8 December 1869. The Ultramontane bishops were lobbying for a definition of papal infallibility, although that had not been mentioned in the bull convening the Council. But unscrupulous as their methods were, Newman pointed out to the outraged Döllinger that intrigue was a feature of Councils. Unlike the doctrine of the Immaculate Conception, which had been defined by Pope Pius ix in 1854, the question of papal infallibility was a new question. And the Church, which moved 'as a whole', as a communion, had 'no right rudely to wipe out the history of centuries', for 'we are not ripe yet for the Pope's Infallibility'. To force a dogma in this surreptitious way on the Church was 'crooked'. Extensive historical research and theological discussion were essential preliminaries. It looked suspiciously as if 'a grave dogmatic question was being treated merely as a move in ecclesiastical politics'. The Ultramontanes 'wished to steal a march upon Catholics. Nothing is above board—nothing is told to the bishops generally before hand—the gravest innovation possible, (for it is a change in the hitherto recognized basis of the Church,) is to be carried by acclamation.' However, Newman still believed that there would be no definition, and that if one were made it would be 'in so mild a form as, practically to mean little or nothing'. Nevertheless, although the Council would be protected by the Holy Spirit from teaching error, it was not divinely prevented from acting inopportunely. But even that eventuality must, Newman thought, be in the long run expedient in God's providence, however inexpedient it might seem at the time.[58]

Hostile as he was to the Ultramontanes, Newman did not agree with liberal Catholics like Döllinger in their absolute opposition to the eventual definition that was passed by the Council. True, he considered it 'a new and most serious precedent in the Church that a dogma...should be passed *without definite and urgent cause*'. However, he was 'pleased at its moderation', the 'terms used' were 'vague', and he personally had no difficulty in accepting it. Quite apart from the authority of the Council—which was in some doubt at first as more than eighty bishops opposed to the definition had left before the vote was taken—for centuries the pope had 'been allowed by God to assert virtually his infallibility'. And then perhaps it was '*necessary*, in time to come, for the seat of government to be strengthened'; if 'terrible times' were imminent, a formal increase in papal authority might be 'absolutely necessary to keep things together'. On the other hand, the effect of the definition might be actually to '*limit* the Pope's power' because its limit was at least now defined. True, it was only for the last three hundred years the Church had 'acted on the doctrine' of papal infallibility, but from the beginning the popes had 'so intervened and interposed in all parts of Christendom, so authoritatively and magisterially' that it was very hard not to believe that they possessed the 'divine gift of direction and teaching'. And what, after all, had the definition added of any 'consequence'? Catholic theologians had always held that 'what the Pope said ex cathedrâ, was true, *when* the Bishops had received it—what has been passed, is to the effect that what he determines ex cathedrâ is true *independently* of the reception by the Bishops—but nothing has been passed as to *what is meant* by "ex cathedrâ"—and this falls back to the Bishops and the Church to determine quite as much as before'. This radical point, of course, cut both ways—against the exaggerated interpretations of the significance and scope of the definition of both Ultramontanes and liberals: there was no real theological justification either for the triumphalism of Cardinal Manning or for the outright rejection of the definition by liberals like Döllinger. Moreover, the definition was only concerned with faith and morals, whereas the Ultramontanes had wanted it to cover 'political principles', in particular to enforce rigorously the notorious Syllabus of Errors. Anyway, Newman himself professed to be an Ultramontane in its original sense as used by Montalembert, who had appealed 'beyond the mountains' (i.e. the Alps) to Rome in his opposition to the Gallican idea of a national Church and the resulting state interference. And while Newman had 'always inclined to the notion that a General Council was the magisterial exponent of the Creed', unfortunately it had to be admitted that 'a General Council may be hampered and hindered by the action of infidel Governments upon a weak or time-serving episcopate'. The argument that papal authority required strengthening was not lost on him: 'It is...better that the individual command of Christ to Peter to teach the nations, and to guard the Christian structure of society, should be committed to his undoubted successor. By this means there will be no more of those misunderstandings out of which Jansenism and Gallicanism have arisen...'. As for Councils, they were 'with few exceptions, a dreary, unlovely phenomenon in the Church'. Indeed, a few years later Newman was even more negative about Councils and correspondingly more positive about the papacy: 'The more one examines the Councils, the less satisfactory they are... [but] the less satisfactory *they*, the more majestic and trust-winning, and the more imperatively necessary, is the action of the Holy See.'[59]

In November 1874 William Gladstone published a pamphlet entitled *The Vatican Decrees in their Bearing on Civil Allegiance: A Political Expostulation*, in which he claimed that Catholics were now subjects of the pope and could no longer be regarded as loyal citizens. Newman welcomed the attack as it would give him the opportunity indirectly to speak out against the extreme Ultramontanes. *The Letter to the Duke of Norfolk*, which was a very long letter, being a book some two hundred pages long, was published in January 1875. As in the last chapter of the *Apologia*, Newman steers a careful course between the rightful demands of authority and the legitimate concerns of theologians. At the outset he emphasizes a point that he had made in a private letter in 1870, namely that the definition of 1870, like all definitions and teachings of Councils and popes, did not speak for itself—it required interpretation by theologians, just as 'lawyers explain acts of Parliament'. Nor could abstract definitions and teachings 'determine particular fact': the doctrine, for instance, that there was no salvation outside the Church did not apply to people in 'invincible ignorance'.[60] It did not follow that 'because there is no Church but one, which has the Evangelical gifts and privileges to bestow, that therefore no one can be saved without the intervention of that one Church', for it was 'possible to belong to the soul of the Church without belonging to the body'. In the case of the traditional teaching on usury, words had changed their meaning in very different economic circumstances from those that prevailed when the teaching was first promulgated, with the result that the teaching was no longer applicable in practice. These two instances alone showed 'what caution is to be observed' in interpreting Church teachings. But, on the other hand, because abstract or general doctrines could not be divorced from concrete contexts, it did not follow that condemnations of 'the very wording' of particular propositions did not involve infallibility, since otherwise 'neither Pope nor Council could draw up a dogmatic

---

[59]   *LD* xxv.164, 170, 175, 200, 224, 259; xxvi.120; xxviii.172.
[60]   *LD* xxv.71.

definition at all, for the right exercise of words is involved in the right exercise of thought'. Still, the 'definite rules' and 'traditional principles of interpretation' necessary for interpreting definitions were 'as cogent and unchangeable' as the definitions themselves. Of great importance was the 'principle of minimizing', whereby theologians explain 'in the concrete' a teaching of the magisterium 'by strict interpretation of its wording, by the illustration of its circumstances, and by the recognition of exceptions'. This 'legitimate minimizing' takes advantage on the one hand of the 'intensely concrete character of the matters condemned' in 'negative' condemnations, and on the other hand of the abstract nature of 'affirmative' definitions of doctrine, which 'admit of exceptions in their actual application'. But if Newman is anxious to mitigate the exaggerations of the Ultramontanes, he is also unequivocal in his criticism of the liberal Döllinger and his followers. While it 'is a tragical event, both for them and for us, that they have left us,' he wrote, 'I think them utterly wrong in what they have done and are doing; and, moreover, I agree as little in their view of history as in their acts'. It was not a matter of questioning the accuracy of their historical knowledge, but 'their use of the facts they report' and 'that special stand-point from which they view the relations existing between the records of History and the communications of Popes and Councils'—'They seem to me to expect from History more than History can furnish'. The opposite was true of the Ultramontanes, who simply dismissed history as irrelevant:

> As the Church is a sacred and divine creation, so in like manner her history, with its wonderful evolution of events, the throng of great actors who have a part in it, and its multiform literature, stained though its annals are with human sin and error, and recorded on no system, and by uninspired authors, still is a sacred work also; and those who make light of it, or distrust its lessons, incur a grave responsibility.

As for Döllinger the Church historian, Newman wondered why 'private judgment' should be 'unlawful in interpreting Scripture against the voice of authority, and yet be lawful in the interpretation of history?' The Church certainly made use of history, as she also used Scripture, tradition, and human reason; but her doctrines could not be 'proved' by any of these 'informants', individually or in combination. No Catholic doctrine could be fully proved (or, for that matter, disproved) by historical evidence—'in all cases there is a margin left for the exercise of faith in the word of the Church'. Indeed, anyone 'who believes the dogmas of the Church only because he has reasoned them out of History, is scarcely a Catholic.'[61]

6

In 1877 Newman republished his Anglican *Lectures on the Prophetical Office of the Church* together with a lengthy new preface. He wanted to correct his mistake in blaming corruptions in the Church on Catholic theology: 'ambition, craft, cruelty, and superstition are not commonly the characteristic of theologians', he pointed out, but in fact 'bear on their face the marks of having a popular or a political origin', and 'theology, so far from encouraging them, has restrained and corrected such extravagances as have been committed...in the exercise of the regal and sacerdotal powers'. Indeed, the Church was never 'in greater danger than when...the Schools of theology have been broken up and ceased to be'.

> I say, then, Theology is the fundamental and regulating principle of the whole Church system. It is commensurate with Revelation, and Revelation is the initial and essential idea of Christianity. It is the subject-matter, the formal cause, the expression, of the Prophetical Office, and, as being such, has created both the Regal Office and the Sacerdotal. And it has in a certain sense, a power of jurisdiction over these offices, as being its own creations, theologians being ever in request and in employment in keeping within bounds both the political and popular elements in the Church's constitution,—elements which are more congenial than itself to the human mind, are far more liable to excess and corruption...[62]

Newman seems to be speaking with the liberal voice of the *Rambler* of Acton and Simpson, but now another voice is heard: 'Yet theology cannot always have its own way; it is too hard, too intellectual, too exact, to be always equitable, or to be always compassionate...' Popular religion may, for example, reject a more accurate translation of the Bible because to 'the devotional mind what is new and strange is as repulsive, often as dangerous, as falsehood is to the scientific'. More seriously, there was the possibility of a conflict between 'religious inquiry or teaching' and 'investigation in purely secular matters'. There was a modern assumption that whenever there was an

---

[61] *Diff.* ii.335, 337, 330, 280, 332, 321, 334, 309, 311–12.
[62] *VM* ii.xlvii–xlviii, lii.

apparent (and only apparent) contradiction between religion and science, then religion must immediately give way. But even though Galileo was 'right in his conclusion that the earth moves' and though it 'might have been wrong' to condemn him as a heretic, nevertheless 'there was nothing wrong in censuring abrupt, startling, unsettling, unverified disclosures...when the limits of revealed truth had not as yet been verified'. Newman finds the contrast between theology and popular religion in the Gospels themselves, citing the case of the woman with the haemorrhage who hoped to be cured by touching the cloak of Jesus, who 'passed over the superstitious act' and healed her because of her faith. In fact, he praised her for 'what might, not without reason, be called an idolatrous act'. Indeed, in the Gospels the 'idolatry of ignorance' is superior to other idolatries (that of wealth, for example), which, however, are not 'commonly startling or shocking to educated minds'. Where was there an instance of Jesus condemning superstition? But such incidents in the Gospels 'form an aspect of the Apostolic Christianity very different from that presented by St. Paul's Pastoral Epistles and the Epistle General of St. John'.[63]

7

In 1878 Newman delivered in Rome his famous *biglietto* speech following his elevation to the College of Cardinals. He began by referring to the 'many trials' he had suffered, a clear reference to his persecution by the Ultramontanes for his alleged liberal Catholicism. In fact, the 'one great mischief' he had opposed 'from the first' was 'the spirit of liberalism in religion'.

> Liberalism in religion is the doctrine that there is no positive truth in religion, but that one creed is as good as another...It is inconsistent with any recognition of any religion, as *true*. It teaches that all are to be tolerated, for all are matters of opinion. Revealed religion is not a truth, but a sentiment and a taste; not an objective fact...

But he does not hesitate in the heart of papal Rome to introduce the important modification, 'that there is much in the liberalistic theory which is good and true; for example.... the precepts of justice, truthfulness'. But then it is precisely because of the positive side of

---

[63] *VM* i.xlviii, liii, lv, lxvi–lxviii.

liberalism that 'There never was a device of the Enemy, so cleverly framed, and with such promise of success.'[64]

Having abandoned the attempt as a Tractarian Anglican to construct a *via media* or middle way between Rome and Geneva, Newman found that he had to forge another *via media* as a Catholic between the Ultramontane and liberal wings of the Church. Neither simply conservative nor liberal, he is best described again as a conservative radical or conservative reformer. Open to development and reform, yet insistent on the tradition and authority of the Church, Newman was himself a proponent of that hermeneutic which is the subject of the next chapter.

---

[64] *Campaign* 393, 395, 398–9.

2

The Hermeneutic of Change in Continuity

1

In what has become a famous speech, Pope Benedict XVI in 2005, at the outset of his pontificate, contrasted two rival interpretations of the Second Vatican Council. On the one hand, there was 'an interpretation' that he 'would call a "hermeneutic of discontinuity and rupture"'; on the other hand, there was 'the "hermeneutic of reform", of renewal in the continuity of the one subject-Church which the Lord has given to us. She is a subject which increases in time and develops, yet always remaining the same.'[1] Or, as the Pope put it five years later: 'The Council did not formulate anything new in matters of faith, nor did it wish to replace what was ancient. Rather, it concerned itself with seeing that the same faith might continue to be lived in the present day…'.[2]

In his *Essay on the Development of Christian Doctrine*, Newman makes exactly the same point when he writes that as a 'fact' which 'impresses an idea of itself on our minds', Christianity '*changes*… in order to remain the *same*' [my italics].[3] This process is what Newman means by development. When, on the other hand, an 'idea' like that of Christianity changes only to become something different, then there

---

[1] Christmas Address to the Roman Curia, 22 December 2005, <http://www.zenit.org/en/articles/pope-s-christmas-address-to-curia--3> Pope Francis has endorsed this hermeneutic of continuity in his letter of 19 November 2013 to Cardinal Walter Müller, papal envoy to the celebration of the 450th anniversary of the close of the Council of Trent, <http://www.zenit.org/en/articles/pope-highlights-continuity-of-tradition-from-trent-to-vatican-ii>

[2] Homily at the opening of the Year of Faith, 11 October 2012, <http://www.zenit.org/en/articles/pope-benedict-s-homily-at-opening-mass-of-the-year-of-faith>

[3] *Dev.* 40, 55.

is not development but 'corruption'. 'I venture', Newman writes, 'to set down seven Notes of varying cogency, independence and applicability, to discriminate healthy developments of an idea from its state of corruption and decay'. These seven 'notes', then, which he called 'tests' in the first edition of the *Essay*, are, by his own admission, only 'seven out of various Notes, which may be assigned, of fidelity in the development of an idea'.[4] But are they of any real value?

According to Owen Chadwick, they were only 'half-heartedly' proposed by Newman, 'convinced no one', and were 'once admitted [by Newman] to be incapable of performing their ostensible purpose'.[5] Chadwick fails to give any reference to where Newman made this admission, an admission which would flatly contradict his repeated insistence, first in the 1845 edition of the *Essay on Development*, that 'rules are required to distinguish legitimate developments from those which are not such';[6] then sixteen years later in 1861 'that no one can religiously speak of development, without giving the *rules* which keep it from extravagating endlessly': 'And I give seven tests of a true development... These tests secure the substantial immutability of Christian doctrine';[7] and finally in the revised edition of the *Essay* in 1878 that it was 'necessary... to assign certain characteristics of faithful developments, which none but faithful developments have, and the presence of which serves as a test to discriminate between them and corruptions'.[8] Since in any case Newman spends some thirty-five pages elaborating these 'notes' or 'tests', and the rest of the book, of over two hundred pages, applying them to Christianity, it seems somewhat strange, to say the least, that he should have been half-hearted about them, regarding them as useless.

Similarly, Nicholas Lash dismisses the notes as means of evaluating whether a change is a development or a corruption:

> If we looked there, we should be disappointed. It is true that, taken together, the tests do have a certain coherence. But they are not (as they have often taken to be) general criteria for distinguishing sound from

[4] *Dev.* 205–6.
[5] Owen Chadwick, *From Bossuet to Newman* (Cambridge: Cambridge University Press, 1957), 143, 155.
[6] *An Essay on the Development of Christian Doctrine: The Edition of 1845*, ed. J.M. Cameron (Harmondsworth, Middlesex: Penguin Books, 1974), 116.
[7] *LD* xx.54.   [8] *Dev.* 170.

unsound developments. Fundamentally, their purpose is not criteriological, but apologetic.[9]

And Lash quotes Newman in support: 'they rather serve as answers to objections brought against the actual decisions of authority, than are proofs of the correctness of those decisions'.[10] Certainly, Newman was clear that the notes 'are insufficient for the guidance of individuals in the case of so large and complicated a problem as Christianity, though they may aid our inquiries and support our conclusions in particular points. They are of a scientific and controversial, not of a practical character, and are instruments rather than warrants of right decisions'. The warrant for an authentic development was provided not by the notes but by 'an external authority', that is, 'the infallibility of the Church'.[11] But that does not justify Lash's dismissal of the notes as merely 'apologetic' and not 'criteriological', as Newman clearly thought they were, who, as we have seen, saw them as '*rules*' for discerning authentic developments. And in 1990 the Roman Catholic Church's International Theological Commission agreed with Newman that the notes constitute 'a criteriology for dogmatic development...that is useful...for the ongoing contemporary interpretation of dogmas'.[12]

Newman did not think that you could apply the notes and prove by logical demonstration that a particular change was a development or a corruption. However, that did not mean that one could not be certain by applying the notes that a change was a corruption or a development. For, as he was to put it in his *Essay in Aid of a Grammar of Assent*, there are 'many truths in concrete matter, which no one can demonstrate, yet every one unconditionally accepts'.[13] There certainty can be reached by what Newman calls 'the cumulation of probabilities', the '*assemblage* of concurring and converging probabilities'. These 'converging probabilities', put together, are like 'a *cable* which is made up of a number of separate threads, each feeble, yet together as sufficient as an iron rod'—'An iron rod represents mathematical or strict demonstration; a cable represents...an assemblage of probabilities,

---

[9]   Nicholas Lash, *Change in Focus: A Study of Doctrinal Change and Continuity* (London: Sheed and Ward, 1973), 97.

[10]   *Dev.* 78.   [11]   *Dev.* 78.

[12]   *Origins*, 20 (1990), 13. See Gerard H. McCarren, 'Development of Doctrine', in Ian Ker and Terrence Merrigan, eds, *The Cambridge Companion to John Henry Newman* (Cambridge: Cambridge University Press, 2009), 127–8.

[13]   *GA* 106, 187.

separately insufficient for certainty, but, when put together, irrefragable.'[14] In Newman's view, then, the seven notes or tests, when all or most of them point towards corruption or development, may indeed be sufficient to justify certainty that a particular change is a corruption or development. By themselves they do not provide any kind of certainty, but taken together they are capable of doing so. It is surely in that light that we should evaluate the usefulness of the notes,[15] and this is best done by applying them to concrete instances, which is what I propose to do in this chapter, by considering first the *Apologia* and secondly the Second Vatican Council's most controversial document, which most obviously represents either authentic development or a corruption signifying rupture with the Church's tradition. I believe that these two applications of the notes will show that Peter Hinchliff was unduly pessimistic when he wrote that the notes can 'really only be applied in retrospect, and then somewhat uncertainly'.[16]

But before considering whether Newman's theological autobiography can be viewed, in the light of the notes, to be a history of a religious development as opposed to corruption—as the anti-Catholic Protestant public of Victorian England assumed to be the case (at least until the publication of the *Apologia*)—it is necessary to consider some objections to its accuracy and honesty, objections which, if true, would cast doubt on the narrative as a whole.

2

According to Frank M. Turner, Newman deliberately falsified the record in the *Apologia* in maintaining that Tractarianism was essentially a struggle against liberalism: 'what the structure and purpose of Newman's narrative of 1864 by its very nature concealed was his

---

[14] *GA* 106, 187; *Apo.* 31; *LD* xxi.146.

[15] Cf. Avery Cardinal Dulles, SJ, *Newman* (London and New York: Continuum, 2002), 79: 'Newman…would have repudiated the notion that the development of doctrine could be reduced to a set of rules. He did think it possible, however, to propose some rule of thumb that could be applied by the discerning inquirer to distinguish between true developments and corruptions.' Cf. McCarren, 'Development of Doctrine', 128–9.

[16] Peter Hinchliff, *God and History: Aspects of British Theology 1875–1914* (Oxford: Clarendon Press, 1992), 44.

antipathy...to evangelical Protestantism, a dislike bordering on hatred that had been the single most energizing force in his thought and theology during the 1830s and early 1840s'. Turner claims that Newman 'assiduously recast [the] Tractarian assault on evangelical religion into a struggle against liberals and liberalism'.[17] His motive in doing so was, Turner argues, to curry favour with both orthodox Protestants and also especially the authorities in Rome where he was viewed with suspicion as a liberal Catholic.

However, it is by no means clear that Turner understands what was and is meant by Evangelicalism; indeed, he is bizarrely inconsistent in his own definitions. On one occasion he equates it with what he calls 'popular Protestantism'[18]—but the 'popular Protestantism' of Victorian England was certainly not Evangelicalism. Popular Protestantism was the kind of Protestantism we find in the novels of Charles Dickens, who never lost an opportunity to satirize Evangelical clergymen. Evangelicals, high church Anglicans, and liberal Anglicans were, in Newman's words, 'only denominations, parties, schools, compared with the national religion', or 'Bible Religion', which consisted 'not in rites or creeds, but mainly in having the Bible read in Church, in the family, and in private'.[19] As we saw in the previous chapter, of the three 'parties', Newman was clear that it was from the liberal or latitudinarian party that the principal danger came. Bizarrely, elsewhere Turner actually equates liberalism with Evangelicalism: 'Liberalism in religion was evangelical Protestantism...'.[20] But then it is also not clear that Turner understands what was meant by liberalism, which he calls 'secular rationalism or secular critical thought'.[21] It is true, of course, that Newman thought that liberal or latitudinarian theology led ultimately to secular rationalism, but when he insisted that the Oxford Movement was a movement to oppose liberalism he meant the former not the latter. Similarly, it is also true that he held that Evangelicalism tended towards latitudinarianism and worse: 'That system has become rationalistic in Germany, Socinian in Geneva— Socinian among English Presbyterians and Arian among Irish— Latitudinarian in Holland—it tends to Socinianism among our own

[17] Frank M. Turner, *John Henry Newman: The Challenge to Evangelical Religion* (New Haven and London: Yale University Press, 2002), 9.
[18] Turner, *John Henry Newman*, 9.   [19] *GA* 43.
[20] Frank M. Turner, ed., *Apologia pro Vita Sua and Six Sermons* (New Haven and London: Yale University Press, 2008), 63.
[21] Turner, *John Henry Newman*, 10–11.

Evangelical party.'[22] But the liberals the Tractarians were opposing in the Church of England were neither Evangelicals nor secular rationalists but latitudinarians. R.W. Church, the first contemporary historian of the Oxford Movement, in which he had participated, who had no motive for falsifying the record, in his review of the *Apologia* called it 'the history of a great battle against Liberalism, understanding by Liberalism the tendencies of modern thought to destroy the basis of revealed religion.'[23] And Church agreed 'on the whole' with Newman that it was the liberals, who 'supplied the brains', who were responsible for the university's condemnation of *Tract 90* in 1841.[24] Whatever their deficiencies and limitations (about which certainly Newman was unsparing), the truth is that he was by no means simply hostile to Evangelicals, but looked 'most hopefully towards numbers of them—They are a very heterogenous party, but contain some of the highest and noblest elements of the Christian character among them, which have been attracted to the existing system of seriousness and spirituality, defective as it was, since the time that the lowminded' Latitudinarians of the previous century 'robbed the Church of all her more beautiful characteristics'. It was this 'want of deeper views' that had led to 'a large portion of the deepest and truest religious principle' being 'seduced' into a 'school' whose '*spirit*' admittedly tended to liberalism.[25]

Another charge against Newman's account of his theological development in the *Apologia*, which has been voiced by several writers, is that he came to the theory of doctrinal development much later than he claimed. According to Newman in the *Apologia*, he had mentioned 'the principle of development of doctrine' in his 1836 article 'Home Thoughts Abroad', 'and even at an earlier date I had introduced it into my History of the Arians in 1832; nor had I ever lost sight of it in my speculations'. It was, though, only 'at the end of 1842' and at the beginning of 1843 that he 'gave [his] mind' to it and 'began to consider it attentively' as he prepared his February 1843 university sermon on 'The Theory of Developments in Religious Doctrine'.[26]

The concept of development is more implicit than explicit in the *Arians* (completed in 1832 but not published till 1833), as when Newman writes:

---

[22] *LD* vi.133.
[23] R.W. Church, *Occasional Papers* (London: Macmillan, 1897), ii.386.
[24] *LD* xxi.449, n. 5.   [25] *LD* v.21, 32.   [26] *Apo.* 178.

Before the mind has been roused to reflection and inquisitiveness about its own acts and impressions, it acquiesces, if religiously trained, in that practical devotion to the Blessed Trinity, and implicit acknowledgement of the divinity of Son and Spirit, which holy Scripture at once teaches and exemplifies... Moral feelings do not directly contemplate and realize to themselves the objects which excite them... Thus the systematic doctrine of the Trinity may be considered as the shadow, projected for the contemplation of the intellect, of the Object of scripturally-informed piety... given to the Church by tradition contemporaneously with those apostolic writings, which are addressed more directly to the heart; kept in the background in the infancy of Christianity, when faith and obedience were vigorous, and brought forward at a time when, reason being disproportionately developed, and aiming at sovereignty in the province of religion, its presence became necessary to expel an usurping idol from the house of God.[27]

But in 'Home Thoughts Abroad' he had spoken much more explicitly of 'all those necessary developments of the elements of Gospel truth, which could not be introduced throughout the Church except gradually'.[28] However, as we saw in the previous chapter,[29] already by 1834 in a private letter and in *Tract 40* he had already clearly and explicitly grasped the concept of doctrinal development.

And yet according to Aidan Nichols, the concept of doctrinal development 'at last makes its appearance' only in 1837 in *Lectures on the Prophetical Office of the Church*, and then only in an unfavourable reference to the Roman Catholic idea of development.[30] Owen Chadwick puts the date even later, calling the 1843 sermon 'The Theory of Developments in Religious Doctrine' Newman's 'first utterance upon the subject'.[31]

More recently James Pereiro has asserted that 'it is not possible to conclude that [Newman] then [in 1834] held a theory of development'. According to Pereiro, the 'reference to doctrinal development' in *Tract 40* is 'put forward by a layman', who is not necessarily 'expressing Newman's own ideas'.[32] But this is incorrect: the *Laicus* who is receiving instruction from the Tractarian *Clericus*—who is clearly

---

[27] *Ari.* 143, 145.   [28] *DA* 19.   [29] See Chapter 1, section I.3, pp. 9–10.
[30] Aidan Nichols, OP, *From Newman to Congar: The Idea of Doctrinal Development from the Victorians to the Second Vatican Council* (Edinburgh: T & T Clark, 1990), 35.
[31] Chadwick, *From Bossuet to Newman*, 89.
[32] James Pereiro, *'Ethos' and the Oxford Movement: At the Heart of Tractarianism* (Oxford: Oxford University Press, 2008), 165.

Newman—is expressing not his own view but that of *Clericus*: 'I think I quite understand the ground you take. You consider that...'[33] Pereiro argues that 'even if Laicus were expressing Newman's own ideas (as he later claimed)...For Newman the bosom of the Church was ample and did not contain only dogmatic truth...Prophetical Tradition also found refuge within it...Besides, Laicus's words were perfectly applicable to the *Disciplina Arcani*', that is 'the principle of reserve' or 'economy', which would explain apparent doctrinal developments as the 'late appearance' of 'Christian doctrine hidden from public view'.[34] However, the 1834 letter, of which Pereiro is apparently ignorant, makes it perfectly clear that *Laicus*, who is expressing the view of *Clericus*, is speaking of dogmatic doctrinal developments.

Pereiro cites the view of Louis Allen that when Newman wrote the *Arians*, he had a 'static' idea of doctrine. In fact, Allen, the editor of Newman's public letters to the French Abbé Jager in their controversy of 1834–5, only maintains that in Newman's 'early work' development 'is *usually* [my italics] an attribute of "Romanism", in other words it is a case *against* which he argues'. For what is clear in these letters is that Newman is fully alive to doctrinal development, but distinguishes between his own and the Roman view of it. He accepts that the Church, or branches of it, have the 'power to develop its fundamental Creed into Articles of religion...not however as necessary to be believed for communion', although 'If made by the whole Church in early times, and professing to come from Apostolic tradition, they will come with great weight to all Christians in every age'. The Anglican view is that only the so-called 'fundamentals are the conditions of communion', which are contained in the Creed which in turn is based on Scripture. But Newman also accepts that these fundamental articles of the Creed were 'explained and developed under all forms in the century of the Apostles and since'. What, however, he cannot accept is the Roman view that 'articles defined and accumulated by the Church in the course of centuries, however true they may be' are also necessary for communion. And yet at the same time he speaks of the Church as 'the pillar and ground of the truth, of Christian truth in all its *developments* [my italics]', requiring her members to 'subscribe not only to the words of the Apostles' Creed but also to the particular sense she attached to them'—presumably partly at least because

---

[33] *VM* ii.40.   [34] Pereiro, *'Ethos' and the Oxford Movement*, 165.

of 'developments'.[35] To say that Newman did not believe in doctrinal development because he rejected the Roman concept of it would be like saying that as a Tractarian he did not believe in the Real Presence in the Eucharist, when he manifestly did, and believed it to be the faith of the Apostolic Church, because he rejected the Tridentine doctrine of Transubstantiation.

A similar objection may be made to Pereiro's argument that it is 'unlikely' that Newman believed in doctrinal development in 1834 when 'some months later' he would deny it 'so emphatically'. Here Pereiro is referring partly to a letter that Newman's friend and fellow Tractarian S.F. Wood wrote to Newman on 1 January 1836, but more particularly to a letter he sent Henry Edward Manning on 29 January 1836, in which Wood reports that:

> Newman holds that from the time the Church ceased to be One, the right of any part of it to propound *Articles of faith*, as such, is suspended...Further, he says that before the Reformation the Church never *deduced* any doctrine from Scripture, and by inference blames our Reformers for doing so...Generally, his result is, not merely to *refer* us to antiquity but to *shut us up* in it, and to deprive...the Church, of all those doctrines of Scripture not fully commented on by the Fathers: and he seems to consider that our Reformed Church has erred as much in one direction as the Council of Trent in another...[36]

But all that this letter in fact shows is that Newman considered that no development of doctrine was any longer possible in any branch of the divided Church, and that the Reformed Churches, in particular, had no right to deduce a doctrine like that of justification by faith from Scripture. Far from denying doctrinal development in the early undivided Church, Newman merely held that 'the right' to do so by any branch of the divided Church was 'suspended'. There is nothing in the letter to indicate that he did not believe either in the fact or the theory of doctrinal development.

Finally, Stephen Thomas has questioned Newman's account of how for the first time in the summer of 1839 he began to have serious doubts about the Anglican *via media*. He was studying the

---

[35] Louis Allen, ed., *John Henry Newman and the Abbé Jager: A Controversy on Scripture and Tradition (1834–1836)* (London: Oxford University Press, 1975), 12–13, 40, 80, 85, 89.
[36] Pereiro, *'Ethos' and the Oxford Movement*, 165, 248–9.

Monophysite heresy and he became 'seriously alarmed' at the analogy that history seemed to present to him:

> My stronghold was Antiquity; now here, in the middle of the fifth century, I found, as it seemed to me, Christendom of the sixteenth and the nineteenth centuries reflected. I saw my face in that mirror, and I was a Monophysite. The Church of the *Via Media* was in the position of the Oriental communion, Rome was, where she now is; and the Protestants were the Eutychians.

Newman was also struck by 'the great power of the Pope (as great as he claims now almost)' at the Council of Chalcedon.[37] And, to an imagination acutely sensitive to analogies, the sight of Pope Leo the Great upholding the orthodox doctrine, while the heretics divided into an extreme and a moderate party, was extremely disturbing. However, Newman's failure to 'support' what Thomas calls 'this splendid piece of self-dramatisation by any corroboration of letters or memoranda of the time—something he always does in the *Apologia* when he can', 'provokes suspicion' that he is reading into the past what he only came later to express 'in the forms of his distinctively Roman Catholic rhetoric'.[38] But Thomas ignores the fact that Newman, as the leader of the Oxford Movement, had an obligation not to broadcast the disturbing news and so unsettle his followers about a shock which might prove to be merely transitory. In any case, Newman *did* share his disquiet with his closest friend at the time, Frederic Rogers, writing on 22 September 1839 that 'the whole history of the Monophysites has been a sort of alterative [a medicine which produces alteration in the processes of nutrition]'.[39] Another close friend and former pupil, Henry Wilberforce, remembered how at the beginning of October 1839 Newman had confided to him that 'the position of St. Leo in the Monophysite controversy' had opened 'a vista...to the end of

---

[37]   *LD* vii. 105.

[38]   Stephen Thomas, *Newman and Heresy: The Anglican Years* (Cambridge: Cambridge University Press, 1991), 205–6. Benjamin John King, *Newman and the Alexandrian Fathers: Shaping Doctrine in Nineteenth-century England* (Oxford: Oxford University Press, 2009), 162, appears to share Thomas's 'suspicion': 'the connection that Newman claims to have seen thereafter...between the Donatist–Anglican analogy and Monophysitism, hardly appears in Newman's work at the time'. Unsurprisingly, Turner, ever anxious to cast doubt on Newman's narrative in the *Apologia*, praises Thomas for 'so cogently' arguing against 'accepting' Newman's version of events (*John Henry Newman*, 335).

[39]   *LD* vii.154.

which I do not see.'[40] And Thomas himself admits that in a manuscript paper, dated 23 August 1839, entitled 'The Monophysite Heresy', 'The sense that Newman might have been, as early as 1839, beginning unhappily to find points of correspondence between himself and the Monophysites emerges most clearly in the opening pages...'[41]

3

More than two years after Newman had been received into the Roman Catholic Church, the young Edward White Benson, the future Archbishop of Canterbury, went to hear him preach in St Chad's Cathedral, Birmingham. Benson was deeply impressed, yet also deeply repelled.

> He is a wonderful man truly, and spoke with a sort of Angelic eloquence...Sweet, flowing, unlaboured language in short, very short and very pithy and touching sentences...he was very much emaciated, and when he began his voice was very feeble, and he spoke with great difficulty, nay sometimes he gasped for breath; but his voice was very sweet...it was awful—the terrible lines deeply ploughed all over his face, and the craft that sat upon his retreating forehead and sunken eyes.[42]

It was as though Benson was looking at a fallen Angel, 'a wonderful man truly' but deeply corrupted as 'the craft that sat upon his retreating forehead and sunken eyes' showed only too terribly. In answering Charles Kingsley's charges against him in the *Apologia*, Newman knew that at last he had an opportunity to change the popular image of him as a great man but a man who had somehow been seduced by Rome and corrupted by popery. He could as it were apply his theory of development to his own life to show that there was a deep continuity between the Protestant boy and the Roman Catholic priest.[43]

---

[40] *Moz.* ii.287.   [41] Thomas, *Newman and Heresy*, 206.

[42] A.C. Benson, *The Life of Edward White Benson, Sometime Archbishop of Canterbury* (London: Macmillan, 1899), i.62.

[43] Cf. Dulles, *Newman*, 125: 'It seems fair to say that Newman experienced in himself something analogous to the cumulative process he attributed to the whole Church in his *Essay on the Development of Christian Doctrine*.'

Newman was brought up in a home that typified what he called the 'national religion'[44]. Church of England not chapel, the Newmans were churchgoers, but neither Evangelical nor High Church. Theirs was essentially a Bible religion: 'I was brought up from a child to take great delight in reading the Bible,' Newman remembered, 'but I had no formed religious convictions till I was fifteen. Of course I had a perfect knowledge of my Catechism.' That last sentence is significant, as Newman is saying in effect that to be catechized is not the same as being evangelized—for that conversion is necessary. In Newman's case that conversion would not take place until he was fifteen. In the meantime, Newman steeped himself in the Scriptures. As a Catholic he was to lament the average Catholic's ignorance of them. The Bible, he wrote as a Catholic, was 'the best book of meditations which can be, because it is divine':

> This is why we see such multitudes in France and Italy giving up religion altogether. They have not impressed upon their hearts the life of our Lord and Saviour as given in the Evangelists. They believe merely with the intellect, not with the heart. Argument may overset a mere assent of the reason, but not a faith founded in a personal love for the Object of Faith. They quarrel with their priests, and then they give up the Church. We can quarrel with men, we cannot quarrel with a book.[45]

Or, as Newman put it elsewhere, 'to know Christ is to know Scripture'.[46]

During these early years, Newman recorded years later, he was 'very superstitious, and for some time previous to my conversion used constantly to cross myself on going into the dark'. Where he had got this practice from he had no idea, as he knew nothing about Catholicism. The other strange thing was a drawing of a rosary in his 'first Latin verse-book'. He was not yet ten years old when he did the drawing and could only suppose that he had got the idea from a romance, say, of Mrs Radcliffe or some religious picture. But 'the strange thing is, how, among the thousand objects which meet a boy's eyes, these in particular should so have fixed themselves in my mind, that I made them practically my own'.[47]

The next stage of Newman's religious development took place in 1816, when he was a fifteen-year-old adolescent and 'a great change of thought took place in me. I fell under the influences of a definite creed,

---

[44] See section 2 above, p. 44.   [45] *LD* xxvi.87.   [46] *SN* 230.
[47] *Apo.* 16–17.

and received into my intellect impressions of dogma, which, through God's mercy, have never been effaced or obscured.' What he had read in the Bible and learned from the catechism now become *real* to him in a doctrinal sense. And the 'definite creed' that he now receives clearly satisfies three of his notes of development, that is, 'preservation of type' (his religion doesn't change), 'logical sequence' (his new dogmatic faith follows logically from what he knew from the Bible and the catechism), and 'conservative action upon the past' ('it is an addition which illustrates, not obscures, corroborates, not corrects'[48] all that he already knew from the Bible and the catechism). Nearly fifty years later, Newman was to write: 'From the age of fifteen, dogma has been the fundamental principle of my religion: I know no other religion; I cannot enter into the idea of any other sort of religion; religion, as a mere sentiment, is to me a dream and a mockery.'[49] This fidelity to a dogmatic religion exemplifies Newman's seventh note of authentic development, that of chronic vigour. On the other hand, there was the influence of the Evangelical schoolmaster 'who was the human means of this beginning of divine faith in me'. It was not only Walter Mayers's 'conversations and sermons' that influenced Newman, but also 'the books which he put into my hands, all of the school of Calvin'. The two particular Calvinistic doctrines that Newman imbibed were: first, 'the doctrine of final perseverance', which he 'retained...till the age of twenty-one, when it gradually faded away'; second, the doctrine that 'the converted and the unconverted can be discriminated by man, that the justified are conscious of their state of justification, and that the regenerate cannot fall away'. Both these doctrines were incidental to and unconnected with Newman's conversion to a doctrinal Christianity. These and other Evangelical tenets were finally abandoned by Newman after becoming a fellow of Oriel, particularly as a result of the influence of Edward Hawkins, the Provost, who gave him J.B. Sumner's *Apostolical Preaching Considered in an Examination of St. Paul's Epistles* (1815), which led Newman to reject his 'remaining Calvinism, and to receive the doctrine of Baptismal Regeneration'.[50] These doctrines clearly offend against Newman's seventh note of 'chronic vigour' and were therefore corruptions not developments because of their *'transitory character'*.[51]

---

[48] *Dev.* 200.   [49] *Apo.* 17, 54.   [50] *Apo.* 21.   [51] *Dev.* 205.

In that same autumn of 1816 Newman also read Joseph Milner's *History of the Church of Christ* (1794–1809). Milner was one of the founders of Evangelicalism in the Church of England, but nevertheless his work contained 'long extracts from St. Augustine, St. Ambrose, and the other Fathers' with which Newman was 'nothing short of enamoured': 'I read them as being the religion of the primitive Christians…'. But at the same time that he was reading Milner's extracts from the Fathers he was also reading Thomas Newton's *Dissertations on the Prophecies, which have been remarkably fulfilled, and are at this time fulfilling in the world* (1758), 'and in consequence became most firmly convinced that the Pope was the Antichrist predicted by Daniel, St. Paul, and St. John': 'My imagination was stained by the effects of this doctrine up to the year 1843; it had been obliterated from my reason and judgment at an earlier date; but the thought remained upon me as a sort of false conscience.' The effects of reading Milner and Newton simultaneously, 'each contrary to each', was to plant in the adolescent Newman's mind 'the seeds of an intellectual inconsistency which disabled me for a long course of years'. However, the one belief was a corruption as it lacked the note of 'chronic vigour', for 'after many years of intellectual unrest' the anti-papal prejudice gradually fell away.[52] His love for the Fathers, on the other hand, remained, as we shall see.

The next stage in Newman's religious history was short-lived and on the whole it was a corruption rather than a development. He tells us in the *Apologia* that by 1827, under the influence of the Oriel Noetics, particularly Richard Whately, the author of the famous *Elements of Logic* (1826), in the writing of which Newman had assisted, he had been guilty of 'a certain disdain for Antiquity which had been growing on [him] now for several years':

> It showed itself in some flippant language against the Fathers in [his 1826 articles on Apollonius of Tyana and 'Miracles of Scripture'] in the Encyclopaedia Metropolitana, about whom I knew little at the time, except what I had learnt as a boy from Joseph Milner. In writing on the Scripture Miracles…I had read [Conyers] Middleton on the Miracles of the early Church [the credibility of which Middleton denied], and had imbibed a portion of his spirit.
>
> The truth is, I was beginning to prefer intellectual excellence to moral; I was drifting in the direction of the Liberalism of the day. I was rudely

---

[52] *Apo.* 20.

awakened from my dream at the end of 1827 by two great blows—illness and bereavement.

In the *Apologia* Newman defines religious liberalism as 'false liberty of thought, or the exercise of thought upon matters, in which, from the constitution of the human mind, thought cannot be brought to any successful issue, and therefore is out of place', since 'the truths of Revelation' cannot be subjected to 'human judgment', being 'revealed doctrines which are in their nature beyond and independent of it'.[53] This incipient liberalism was clearly not an authentic development if only because it obviously did not conform to the note of continuity of principles as it was inconsistent with the dogmatic principle. However, Newman was only 'drifting' towards not sliding into liberalism—'Even when I was under Dr. Whately's influence, I had no temptation to be less zealous for the great dogmas of the faith, and at various times I used to resist such trains of thought on his part as seemed to me (rightly or wrongly) to obscure them'.[54]

Years later, however, Newman acknowledged an important debt to Whately, and in doing so acknowledged a debt to this period of his life when he came under liberal influences. For Whately had undoubtedly exerted 'an intellectual influence' over him and left 'a mark upon his mind'. Whately, who was 'an original thinker' and whose 'great satisfaction was to find a layman who had made a creed for himself', declaring that he was 'well inclined to a heretic, for his heresy at least showed that he had exercised his mind',[55] had taught Newman the importance of a critical theology. That this was an authentic development is shown by the note of 'chronic vigour'. For, as we have seen,[56] many years later in 1877 Newman was to write as a Catholic that theology was 'the fundamental and regulating principle of the whole Church system', being 'commensurate with Revelation…. the initial and essential idea of Christianity'; while theologians were required to keep in check 'both the political and popular elements in the Church's constitution', which were particularly 'liable to excess and corruption'.[57] This was a development that also satisfied the note of preservation of type: Newman had been thinking about theological matters since his 1816 conversion. Nor did it offend against the note of continuity of principles, since being critical theologically is not the same

---

[53] *Apo.* 256.   [54] *Apo.* 54–5.   [55] *AW* 70–1.
[56] See Chapter 1, section II.6, p. 37.   [57] *VM* i.xlvii–xlviii.

as being anti-dogmatic. It also seems clearly to satisfy the notes of the power of assimilation and conservative action, for Newman assimilates a new element but does so without contradicting or reversing 'the course of doctrine which has [already] been developed'.[58]

In the *Apologia* Newman writes: 'In proportion as I moved out of the shadow of that liberalism which had hung over my course, my early devotion towards the Fathers returned; and in the long vacation of 1828 I set about to read them chronologically, beginning with St. Ignatius and St. Justin.'[59] The Eastern Father who most influenced Newman was St Athanasius, but he was also influenced by St Basil, St Gregory of Nyssa, St Gregory Nazianzen, and St Cyril of Alexandria.[60] He was attracted too by the thought of St Clement and Origen, 'whose broad philosophy', he wrote, 'carried me away'.[61] So far he had read the Scriptures through the eyes first of a Bible Christian, then of an Evangelical, and most recently in 'the shadow' of liberalism. Now he could discover how those early Christians had read the Bible.

First and foremost there was the sense of Christianity as a mystery, the lack of which Newman came to think was the characteristic of the Arian heresy and modern liberal Protestants. As he wrote in his *Arians of the Fourth Century*:

> If the early Church regarded the very knowledge of the truth as a fearful privilege, much more did it regard that truth itself as glorious and awful; and scarcely conversing about it to her children, shrank from the impiety of subjecting it to the hard gaze of the multitude...Now, we allow ourselves publicly to canvass the most solemn truths in a careless or fiercely argumentative way; truths, which it is as useless as it is unseemly to discuss in public.[62]

Then, secondly, there was the Eastern Fathers' emphasis on 'the authority of Tradition' as opposed to theological speculation.[63] Thirdly, Newman found that, as against the Evangelicals who 'think individuals are justified immediately by the great Atonement—justified by Christ's death and not, as St. Paul says, by means of His Resurrection'[64]—the Fathers were clear that 'those who omit the Resurrection in their view of the divine economy, are as really defective in faith as if they omitted

---

[58] *Dev.* 199.   [59] *Apo.* 35.
[60] In the following discussion of the influence of the Greek Fathers on Newman I have adapted material from my *Newman and the Fullness of Christianity* (Edinburgh: T & T Clark, 1993), 84–98.
[61] *Apo.* 36.   [62] *Ari.* 136.   [63] *Ath.* ii.51.   [64] *Jfc.* 174.

the Crucifixion. On the Cross He paid the debt of the world, but as He could not have been crucified without first taking flesh, so again He could not...apply His Atonement without first rising again.'[65]

And so, fourthly, Newman found in the Fathers the role of the Holy Spirit in Christ's redemption. For 'Christ's bodily presence, which was limited to place' had to be 'exchanged for the manifold spiritual indwelling of the Comforter within us'. The Son returned to the Father at the Resurrection, and at Pentecost in his place came 'the eternal Love whereby the Father and the Son have dwelt in each other',[66] in other words the Holy Spirit, whose 'coming is so really His coming, that we might as well say that He was not here in the days of His flesh, when He was visibly in this world, as deny that He is here now, when He is here by His Divine Spirit.'[67] The theology of the Holy Spirit that Newman preached in a great passage like this from the *Parochial and Plain Sermons* is that of the Greek Fathers:

> [Christ] was born of the Spirit, and we too are born of the Spirit. He was justified by the Spirit, and so are we. He was pronounced the well-beloved Son, when the Holy Ghost descended on Him; and we too cry Abba, Father, through the Spirit sent into our hearts. He was led into the wilderness by the Spirit; He did great works by the Spirit; He offered Himself to death by the Eternal Spirit; He was raised from the dead by the Spirit; He was declared to be the Son of God by the Spirit of holiness on His resurrection; we too are led by the same Spirit into and through this world's temptations; we, too, do our works of obedience by the Spirit; we die from sin, we rise again unto righteousness through the Spirit; and we are declared to be God's sons,—declared, pronounced, dealt with as righteous,—through our resurrection unto holiness in the Spirit...Christ Himself vouchsafes to repeat in each of us in figure and mystery all that He did and suffered in the flesh. He is formed in us, born in us, suffers in us, rises again in us; lives in us; and this not by a succession of events, but all at once: for He comes to us as a Spirit, all dying, all rising again, all living.[68]

In accordance with the Eastern Fathers' careful differentiation of the three persons of the Trinity (see below), Newman emphasizes that the Spirit must not be seen as a replacement or substitute for the Son:

> Let us not for a moment suppose that God the Holy Ghost comes in such sense that God the Son remains away. No; He has not so come that

[65] *Ess.* i.247.   [66] *PS* ii.222, 229.   [67] *PS* vi.126.   [68] *PS* v.139.

Christ does not come, but rather He comes that Christ may come in His coming. Through the Holy Ghost we have communion with Father and Son... The Holy Spirit causes, faith welcomes, the indwelling of Christ in the heart. Thus the Spirit does not take the place of Christ in the soul, but secures that place to Christ.[69]

Fifthly, Newman discovered that the Eastern Fathers were as concerned with the Incarnation as with the Resurrection. Indeed, the two are inseparable, for while through the Incarnation human nature was 'renewed', 'glorious and wonderful beyond our thoughts', so as a result of the Resurrection this same nature was raised up in glory, so that 'Henceforth, we dare aspire to enter into the heaven of heavens, and to live for ever in God's presence, because the first-fruits of our race is already there in the Person of His Only-begotten Son.' In a sermon for Easter Sunday, Newman explains that the Resurrection is implied by the Incarnation: 'Corruption had no power over that Sacred Body, the fruit of a miraculous conception.' In the Resurrection the humanity of Christ was not discarded but was transfigured: 'the Divine Essence streamed forth (so to say) on every side, and environed His Manhood, as in a cloud of glory. So transfigured was His Sacred Body, that He who had deigned to be born of a woman, and to hang upon the cross, had subtle virtue in Him, like a spirit, to pass through the closed doors to His assembled followers.'[70]

Sixthly, Newman's insistence on the 'Divine Sonship' as the key to understanding the identity of Christ shows particularly the influence of the Eastern Fathers. Western theology had traditionally commenced with the one divine nature, and only then moved on secondarily to the distinction of the three persons in the Godhead. The East, on the other hand, has always begun with God as Father. As Father, God therefore has a Son who possesses the same divine nature. The Father also has a Spirit who proceeds from the Father, and who then proceeds from the Father to the Son, possessing the same divine nature as the Father and the Son. Rather than the divine nature taking precedence, the divine nature was seen by the Greek Fathers as existing first of all in God the Father. As Newman put it, 'instead of saying "Father, Son and Spirit, are one substance... they would say "In one God and Father are the Son and Spirit"; the words "One Father" standing not only for the Person of the Father, but connecting that

---

[69] *PS* vi.126.   [70] *PS* ii.142–3.

sole Divine substance which is one with His Person.' Pointing out that no problem was more acute for the early Christians than the apparent discrepancy between professing the oneness of God and belief in the Trinity, Newman wrote:

> Christianity began its teaching by denouncing polytheism as wicked and absurd; but the retort on the part of the polytheist was obvious:— Christianity taught a Divine Trinity: how was this consistent with its profession of a Monarchy?...Catholic theologians met this difficulty both before and after the Nicene Council, by insisting on the unity of origin, which they taught as existing in the Divine Triad, the Son and Spirit having a communicated divinity from the Father, and a personal unity with Him...It was for the same reason that the Father was called God absolutely, while the Second and third Persons were designated by Their personal names of 'the Son', or 'the Word', and 'the Holy Ghost'; viz. because they are to be regarded, not as separated from, but as inherent in the Father.[71]

Writing many years after he had become a Catholic, Newman was insistent that, in spite of the Western Church's wariness of emphasizing the primacy of the Father because of its abuse by the Arians in questioning the divinity of Christ, 'what St. Irenaeus, St. Athanasius, and St. Basil taught, can never be put aside. It is as true now as when those great Fathers enunciated it; and if true, it cannot be ignored without some detriment to the fullness and symmetry of the Catholic dogma.' It was, he thought, of particular importance for understanding the Incarnation:

> One obvious use of it is to facilitate to the imagination the descent of the Divine Nature to the human, as revealed in the doctrine of the Incarnation; the Eternal Son becoming by a second birth the Son of God in time, is a line of thought which preserves to us the continuity of idea in the Divine Revelation, whereas, if we say abruptly that the Supreme Being became the Son of Mary, this, however true when taken by itself, still by reason of the infinite distance between God and man, acts in the direction of the Nestorian error of a Christ with two Persons, as certainly as the doctrine of the *Principatus*, when taken by itself, favours the Arian error of a merely human Christ.[72]

As an Anglican, Newman had made the same point in the more popular language of the preacher:

---

[71] *TT* 167–8, 170–1.   [72] *TT* 178–9.

Our Lord's Sonship is not only the guarantee to us of His Godhead, but also the condition of His incarnation. As the Son was God, so on the other hand was the Son suitably made man; it belonged to Him to have the Father's perfections, it became Him to assume a servant's form. We must beware of supposing that the Persons of the Ever-blessed and All-holy Trinity differ from each other only in this, that the Father is not the Son, and the Son is not the Father. They differ in this besides, that the Father *is* the Father, and the Son *is* the Son. While They are one in substance, Each has distinct characteristics which the Other has not. Surely these sacred Names have a meaning in them, and must not lightly be passed over.[73]

Seventhly, The Greek Fathers understood justifying grace in terms of the deification or divinization of the Christian by virtue of the indwelling of the Holy Spirit, that is, through the Spirit of the Father and the Son. This personal unity with the Trinity is very different from the Western idea of grace as negatively a remedy for sin and as a mere quality of the soul. The doctrine of the indwelling of the Spirit is, of course, in the New Testament, but now Newman was reading it through the eyes of the Eastern Fathers rather than through Evangelical or liberal eyes. And so Newman was able to preach that the Spirit 'pervades us...as light pervades a building, or as a sweet perfume the folds of some honourable robe; so that, in Scripture language, we are said to be in Him, and He in us'. The presence of the Holy Spirit necessarily involves the presence of the Father and the Son, and Newman is emphatic that, invisible as this 'indwelling' is, there is nothing unreal about it: 'we are assured of some real though mystical fellowship with the Father, Son, and Holy Spirit...so that...by a real presence in the soul...God is one with every believer, as in a consecrated Temple'.[74]

In his Anglican *Lectures on the Doctrine of Justification* (1838), Newman proposed a solution to the problem of justification, which of course was at the heart of the Reformation, by invoking the great scriptural and patristic doctrine of the divine indwelling, a doctrine long forgotten and neglected in the Western Church. For surely it was

the great promise of the Gospel, that the Lord of all, who had hitherto manifested Himself externally to His servants, should take up His abode in their hearts...Though He had come in our flesh. So as to be seen and handled, even this was not enough. Still He was external and separate;

---

[73] *PS* vi.58.   [74] *PS* ii.222, 35.

but after His ascension He descended again by and in His Spirit; and then at length the promise was fulfilled.[75]

Our redemption was then complete: the 'dreadful reality' of original sin was overcome by a 'new righteousness', a 'real righteousness' which 'comes from the Holy and Divine Spirit', so that our 'works, done in the Spirit of Christ, have a justifying *principle* in them, and that is the presence of the All-holy Spirit', which 'hallows those acts, that life, that obedience of which it is the original cause, and which it orders and fashions'.[76] Thus the rival Catholic and Protestant theologies of works and faith, both deeply embedded in a late medieval theology of grace, can be circumvented by the rediscovery of the central New Testament doctrine of the indwelling of the Holy Spirit, a doctrine that was second nature to the Eastern Fathers who knew nothing of the sixteenth-century controversy over justification: 'the presence of the Holy Ghost shed abroad in our hearts, the Author both of faith and of renewal, this is really that which makes us righteous, and . . . our righteousness is the possession of that presence'. Justification, then, 'is wrought by the power of the Spirit, or rather by His presence within us', while 'faith and renewal are both present also, but as fruits of it'.[77] The 'connection' between justification and renewal' is that they are 'both included in that one great gift of God, the indwelling of Christ' through the Holy Spirit 'in the Christian soul', which constitutes 'our justification and sanctification, as its necessary results'.[78]

If the answer to the contentious problem of justification is that justification consists in the divine indwelling, then this justification comes through the sacraments. Human flesh was divinized by the Incarnation, and our own personal divinization is achieved sacramentally: 'Our Lord, by becoming man, has found a way whereby to sanctify that nature, of which His own manhood is the pattern specimen. He inhabits us personally, and His inhabitation is effected by the channel of the sacraments'. Through 'this indwelling', Christ is the 'immediate' source of 'spiritual life to each of His elect individually'. Thus, 'while we are in the flesh, soul and body become, by the indwelling of the Word, so elevated above their natural state, so sacred, that to profane them is a sacrilege'.[79]

---

[75] *PS* iv.168.   [76] *PS* v.156–8.   [77] *Jfc.* 137–8.   [78] *Jfc.* 154.
[79] *Ath.* ii.193, 195.

Eighthly, then, Newman's deeply sacramental theology was formed by the writings of the Alexandrian Fathers, from whom he learned of 'the mystical or sacramental principle', according to which 'Holy Church in her sacraments...will remain, even to the end of the world, after all but a symbol of those heavenly facts which fill eternity'.[80] This profoundly sacramental vision meant that Newman never saw the individual sacraments of the Church apart from the *primordial* sacrament, the Church herself. Baptism he understood to be the *primary* sacrament because through it the Christian receives the gift of the Holy Spirit. In a sermon on the words in St Paul's First Letter to the Corinthians, 'By one Spirit are we all baptized into one body', Newman expresses it like this:

> As there is One Holy Ghost, so there is one only visible Body of Christians...and one Baptism which admits men into it. This is implied in the text...But more than this is taught us in it; not only that the Holy Ghost is in the Church, and that Baptism admits into it, but that the Holy Ghost admits by means of Baptism, that the Holy Ghost baptises; in other words, that each individual member receives the gift of the Holy Ghost as a preliminary step, a condition, or means of his being incorporated into the Church; or, in our Saviour's words, that no one can enter, except to be regenerated in order to enter it.[81]

Finally, and ninthly, Newman was again influenced by the Eastern Fathers to see, as he could already have seen for himself from the New Testament, the Church as primarily the communion of those who have received the Holy Spirit through baptism. It was a very different ecclesiology from that of the heavily institutional Tridentine ecclesiology of the Church that he would eventually enter. The Church, he preached as an Anglican, 'is a visible body, invested with, or...existing in invisible privileges', for 'the Church would cease to be the Church, did the Holy Spirit leave it', since 'its outward rites and forms are nourished and animated by the living power which dwells within it'.[82] Indeed, the Church is the Holy Spirit's 'especial dwelling-place'.[83] For while Christ came 'to die for us; the Spirit came to make us one in Him who had died and was alive, that is, to form the Church'. The Church, then, is 'the one mystical body of Christ...quickened by the Spirit'—and it is 'one' by virtue of the Holy Spirit 'giving it *life*'.[84]

---

[80] *Apo.* 36–7.   [81] *PS* iii.271.   [82] *PS* iii.224; v.41.
[83] *PS* iii.270.   [84] *PS* iv.170, 174, 171.

In conclusion, how far are these new changes in Newman's theology authentic developments as opposed to corruptions? They would seem to satisfy every single one of Newman's tests or notes. They illuminate the Scriptures that Newman had read so lovingly if without understanding as a boy, and they therefore evidence the first one, preservation of type. They fully preserve the principle of dogma, and are consequently fully consistent with the second note. They evidently show the power of assimilation in absorbing the teachings of the Fathers, but they do so without disturbing previous developments, instead showing 'a *tendency conservative* of what has gone before'.[85] They are thus consonant with the third and sixth notes. They fulfil the fourth note of logical sequence as Newman, having abandoned Evangelicalism, and turned away from an incipient liberalism, very logically seeks to understand the Scriptures through the eyes of the early Church. The fifth note of anticipation of the future is met in the early enthusiasm of the adolescent Newman for the writings of the Fathers. Finally, the seventh note of chronic vigour is satisfied, as he was to write many years later as a Catholic: 'The Fathers made me a Catholic, and I am not going to kick down the ladder by which I ascended into the Church.'[86]

In 1839 Newman began to have his first doubts about Anglicanism. He became aware of 'the hitch in the Anglican argument'[87]—that, while the Roman Catholic Church could clearly claim Catholicity, the Anglican Church could claim 'Apostolicity'. The Anglican argument that Rome had added to the original apostolic doctrine was undermined by that fact that, for example, the Anglican Church accepted Pope Leo's formulation of the doctrine that Christ was one person with two natures at the Council of Chalcedon several centuries after the time of the Apostles. Here was a clear post-apostolic development of doctrine. If Anglicanism could not be defended without invoking the principle of doctrinal development, how was it possible to object to later developments of doctrine by the Roman Catholic Church? If these were illegitimate accretions and additions, why were those doctrines which Anglicans shared with Roman Catholics, but which were sometimes less clearly to be found in Scripture and the Fathers, not also illegitimate? By the end of 1844 Newman was practically certain that the Church of England, far from being a branch of the Catholic

---

[85] *Dev.* 203.   [86] *Diff.* ii.24.   [87] *Apo.* 138.

Church, was in schism and the Roman Catholic Church was the same Church as the Church of the Fathers. To test his growing conviction, he decided to write *An Essay on the Development of Christian Doctrine* (1845), which he left unfinished on his reception into the Roman Catholic Church in October 1845.

The basic historical fact with which Newman begins is the sheer extent of change in Christianity over the centuries. The question then naturally arises: has there been any 'real continuity of doctrine' since the age of the Apostles? Newman's answer is that, if Christianity is a living idea, then it necessarily grows into 'a body of thought', which will 'after all be little more than the proper representative of one idea, being in substance what that idea meant from the first, its complete image as seen in a combination of diversified aspects, with the suggestions and corrections of many minds, and the illustration of many experiences'. It is 'the process...by which the aspects of an idea are brought into consistency and form', which Newman calls 'its development, being the germination and maturation of some truth or apparent truth on a large mental field'. But 'this process will not be a development, unless the assemblage of aspects, which constitute its ultimate shape, really belongs to the idea from which they start'.[88]

In order to tell whether changes in Christian doctrine are developments or corruptions, then there must be some means of authenticating genuine developments, and so there is, Newman argues, 'a strong antecedent argument in favour of a provision in the Dispensation for putting a seal of authority upon [authentic] developments'. For 'a revelation is not given, if there be no authority to decide what it is that is given'. And so, in order to distinguish true from false developments, a 'supreme authority' is needed.[89] But since the great schism between the Western and Eastern Churches, only the Roman Catholic Church has both developed doctrinally and claimed to have the authority to validate the developments. Newman's conclusion is that there is undeniably a 'very strong presumption' that, 'if there must be and are in fact developments in Christianity, the doctrines propounded by successive Popes and Councils...are they'.[90]

Newman's fundamental reason, then, for converting to the Roman Catholic Church was the necessity for development and the authority needed to authenticate such development. The seven tests or notes

---

[88] *Dev.* 5, 38.   [89] *Dev.* 79, 89.   [90] *Dev.* 96.

that Newman tentatively proposed for distinguishing corruptions from developments did not remove the need for such an authority.

Now it could be argued that *prima facie* Newman's conversion constituted a corruption rather than a development. For, after all, he was entering a Church where lay people were not encouraged to read the Scriptures, where the study of the Fathers was almost non-existent, and where, thanks to the destruction of the theological schools by the French Revolution and the rise of extreme Ultramontanism within the Church, a critical theology was hardly appreciated or welcomed. These defects, however, were not intrinsic to Catholicism, but rather accidental and temporary corruptions of it. So, if we disregard these unwelcoming aspects of the nineteenth-century Church that Newman entered in 1845, how far can we say that his conversion was a theological development rather than corruption?

According to the first note of preservation of type, Newman's conversion to Roman Catholicism was a genuine development, for, as he always used to say to inquirers, he became a Catholic because he became convinced that, in spite of all the obvious changes, the modern Roman Catholic Church was the same Church as that of the Fathers:

> Now the very reason I became a Catholic was because the present Roman Catholic Church is *the only Church* which is like, and it is very like, the primitive Church … It is almost like a photograph of the primitive Church; or at least it does not differ from the primitive Church near so much as the photograph of a man of 40 differs from his photograph when 20. *You know that it is the same man.*[91]

There was clearly no abandonment of the dogmatic principle, so the second note was present. The third note too was satisfied as Roman Catholicism was assimilated into what Newman already believed. Since Newman's conversion to Rome was the result of his study of the Fathers and the early Church there was a logic in his conversion. His childhood practice of crossing himself when going into the dark and his drawing of a rosary could be said to be curious anticipations of the 1845 conversion. It is true that conversion meant the abandonment of the branch theory of the Church and his charges against Rome, but otherwise there was no contradiction or reversal of 'the course of doctrine' which had already been developed.[92] As he was to write more than forty years later, 'those great and burning truths' which

---

he had learned in 1816 'I have found impressed upon my heart with fresh and ever increasing force by the Holy Roman Church', which had 'added' to them but 'obscured, diluted, enfeebled, nothing' of them.[93] The sixth note was also therefore satisfied. The seventh note of chronic vigour was obviously satisfied by the fact that Newman died a Catholic. As he was to write even in the darkest period of his life as a Catholic, he had never 'had one moment's wavering of trust in the Catholic Church', and he would indeed 'be a consummate fool (to use a mild term)' if in his old age he were to leave ' "the land flowing with milk and honey" for the city of confusion and the house of bondage.'[94]

4

According to John Courtney Murray, the theological architect of the Second Vatican Council's Declaration on Religious Liberty (*Dignitatis Humanae*), it 'was, of course, the most controversial document of the whole Council, largely because it raised with sharp emphasis the issue that lay continually below the surface of all the conciliar debates—the issue of the development of doctrine.'[95] This was explicitly acknowledged in the Declaration itself when it says that 'it intends to develop the teaching of recent popes' (art. 1). How far, then, can one say that the document passes Newman's seven tests of notes of authentic development?[96]

The first and most important criterion—not that Newman says it is but it is the one to which he devotes easily the most space—is

---

[93] *LD* xxxi.189. Cf. Dulles, *Newman*, 125: 'His conversion…was not a repudiation but an affirmation and completion of his past; it was continuous, progressive, and incremental.'

[94] *LD* xx.215–16.

[95] *The Documents of Vatican II*, ed. Walter M. Abbott, SJ (London: Geoffrey Chapman, 1966), 673.

[96] The following is an adapted and revised version of my article 'Is *Dignitatis Humanae* a Case of Authentic Doctrinal Development?', *Logos*, 11:2 (Spring 2008), 149–57. For a similar attempt to illustrate 'the enduring value of Newman's seven criteria' (p. 352), see Gerald O'Collins SJ, 'Newman's Seven Notes: The Case of the Resurrection', in Ian Ker and Alan G. Hill, eds, *Newman after a Hundred Years* (Oxford: Clarendon Press, 1990), 337–52. However, O'Collins is there considering a possible future development, whereas Newman saw his tests or notes as applicable to 'the actual decisions of authority' (*Dev*. 78), in other words to a promulgated teaching such as that of *Dignitatis Humanae*.

'preservation of type'. He is careful to acknowledge that this does not rule out 'all variation, nay, considerable alteration of proportion and relation, as time goes on, in the parts or aspects of an idea'. In fact, he argues, appearances may be deceptive since 'real perversions and corruptions are often not so unlike externally to the doctrine from which they come, as are changes which are consistent with it and true developments'.[97] The fact, then, that *Dignitatis Humanae* may appear to contradict previous teaching does not in itself mean it is not a genuine development. Before the Second Vatican Council, the condemnation of religious liberty meant that people were not free to choose whatever religion they pleased. And it is this false 'idea' of religious freedom that is also rejected by *Dignitatis Humanae*, when it declares that the 'one true religion subsists in the catholic and apostolic Church'; and that 'all men are bound to seek the truth...and to embrace the truth...and to hold fast to it'. It also 'professes its belief that it is upon the human conscience that these obligations fall and exert their binding force' (art. 1). Nowhere does the document speak about 'freedom of conscience', implying that a person has the right to do whatever their conscience tells them to do, simply because their conscience tells them to. Consciences can be erroneous and need to be informed, or as the Declaration puts it: 'every man has the duty...to seek the truth in matters religious, in order that he may with prudence form for himself right and true judgments of conscience, with the use of all suitable means' (art. 3). Accordingly, *Dignitatis Humanae* is unambiguous in its conclusion: namely, that the true idea of religious freedom which the Council intends to teach 'leaves untouched traditional Catholic doctrine on the moral duty of men and societies towards the true religion and towards the one Church of Christ' (art. 1). Had the Council failed to embrace the idea of religious freedom expressed in *Dignitatis Humanae*, there would have been a very real danger of a corruption arising in Catholic theology, since, as Newman points out, 'one cause of corruption...is the refusal to follow the course of doctrine as it moves on, and an obstinacy in the notions of the past'.[98] In 1858 he had congratulated Acton on an article on 'the kind of individual liberty which the Catholic doctrine of conscience demanded, a freedom which was better observed in Protestant England than in some Catholic countries'.[99] There the doctrine had been neglected in

---

[97] *Dev.* 173, 176.   [98] *Dev.* 177.
[99] Ian Ker, *John Henry Newman: A Biography* (Oxford: Clarendon Press, 1988), 474.

favour of the Church's teaching on the truth of the Catholic religion and the obligation of people to seek and embrace it. The classical doctrine of conscience, as held by St Thomas Aquinas, for example, was fully recognized in the Council's Constitution on the Church in the Modern World, *Gaudium et Spes*; and had there been a refusal to promulgate *Dignitatis Humanae*, then the Council would have been guilty of 'an obstinacy in the notions of the past'. It was the Council's job to uphold and reconcile *both* doctrines, to distinguish indifferentism from freedom.

As for the second test or note of continuity of principles, Newman, recognizing that the difference between doctrines and principles sometimes depends on how we look at them, argues that the 'life of doctrines may be said to consist in the law or principles which they embody'.[100] Here two principles seem to be relevant. The first is that at any moment in her history certain aspects of what Newman called the Christian 'idea' are inevitably stressed more than others. Thus before the Second Vatican Council the Crucifixion, especially as represented in the sacrifice of the Mass, eclipsed the Resurrection, whereas since the Council there has been a very strong swing of the pendulum the other way. The Church must constantly be seeking to balance the different 'aspects' without excessive imbalances. In the case of religious freedom two doctrines are involved: the duty of all human beings to seek the true religion which is Catholicism, and on the other hand the sovereignty of conscience. *Dignitatis Humanae* would seem, in holding both doctrines, to be a good example of this principle in practice. The second principle is that the Church has to take account of changing circumstances and to apply her doctrines accordingly. For instance, the traditional condemnation of usury surely still holds and is very applicable in societies like India where bond-labourers are to be found. But in economic conditions where lending money is not a form of exploitation but mutually beneficial to both parties, the Church was forced to recognize that the mere physical act of lending money was not the same as what was meant by usury. Similarly, it has come to be seen that the Church's condemnation of contraception applies to the marital act and not to rape.[101] In the case of religious freedom, the first of the two doctrines stated above was assumed in a totally Catholic context like Italy to require the legal exclusion of all

---

[100] *Dev.* 178.   [101] See Chapter 5, section 3, p. 123–4.

other erroneous religions, if only to ensure that, as the Declaration itself allows for, 'the just requirements of public order are observed' (art. 2). Nevertheless, Newman recognized that even in the nineteenth century Italy was less than completely Catholic and that the Church would be better off not using coercion through legal and political means. In a pluralist society the Church does not have the power to impose its will and has to interpret the doctrine in a different way from that of Pio Nono.

Regarding the third note, the 'power of assimilation' or the 'unitive power', *Dignitatis Humanae* in its opening paragraph explicitly recognizes that the Council is responding to external influences when it refers to the growing sense of the dignity of the human person and the importance of responsible freedom as opposed to state coercion. In other words, the Church is willing to absorb ideas emanating from secular thought without fear of compromising her own essential doctrines. Or, as Newman put it, 'The idea never was that throve and lasted, yet…incorporated nothing from external sources'. And certainly, he maintained, the Catholic Church 'can consult expedience more freely than other bodies, as trusting to her living tradition, and is sometimes thought to disregard principle and scruple, when she is but dispensing with forms'.[102]

The Declaration seems also easily to pass the fourth test of 'logical sequence'. This does not necessarily mean 'a conscious reasoning from premises to conclusion'. All that is required is that a doctrine should seem to be 'the *logical issue*' of the 'original teaching'. [103] The original teaching was that Catholicism is the true religion and that all human beings are bound in conscience to embrace it. But *Dignitatis Humanae* points out that 'The truth cannot impose itself except by virtue of its own truth', and that accordingly religious freedom is 'necessary to fulfil' the 'duty' of adhering to the true religion (art. 1). In other words, to follow one's conscience and fulfil one's duty one has to have the freedom to do so. After all, as the Declaration points out, 'It is one of the major tenets of Catholic doctrine that man's response to God must be free' (art. 10) .And even though it admits that 'there have at times appeared ways of acting which were less in accord with the spirit of the Gospel', nevertheless 'the doctrine of the Church that no one is to be coerced into faith has always stood firm' (art. 12).

---

[102] *Dev.* 185, 186, 189.   [103] *Dev.* 189, 195.

The Declaration implicitly invokes Newman's fifth note, that is, 'anticipation of the future', whereby 'definite specimens of advanced teaching…very early occur, which in the historical course are not found till a late day'. For it would be hard to imagine a better example of 'such early…intimations of tendencies which afterwards are fully realized'[104] than the example of Jesus Christ himself, who 'bore witness to the truth, but…refused to impose the truth by force on those who spoke against it' (art. 11). And *Dignitatis Humanae* shows also how this example was followed by his Apostles.

Newman's sixth test or note of an authentic development of doctrine is that of 'conservative action upon its past'. Such is a development 'which is conservative of the course of antecedent developments being really those antecedents and something besides them; it is an addition which illustrates, not obscures, corroborates, not corrects, the body of thought from which it proceeds', 'a *tendency conservative* of what has gone before'.[105] Discussion of the first note has already shown that *Dignitatis Humanae* preserves the two teachings that human beings are not free to choose whatever religion they choose but that they have a duty to seek and hold the true religion, and that the true religion is to be found in the Catholic Church. The Declaration only *seemed* to be a departure from the previous teaching because of the way it was taken to apply in a homogeneous Catholic context. But the teaching is one thing, its interpretation and implementation another. The essential teaching has been preserved and therefore the Declaration passes Newman's sixth test.

As for the seventh and final note of 'chronic vigour' ('*duration* is another test of a faithful development'),[106] *Dignitatis Humanae* would seem clearly to pass this test if some fifty years are anything to go by. True, there are still Lefebvrists who reject it as contrary to the constant teaching and tradition of the Church, but the Church as a whole has received the teaching as authentic and any reversal of it seems quite impossible. St Augustine's knock-down argument against the Donatists in North Africa was 'Securus judicat orbis terrarum'. They were words that had struck Newman with such force in the critical summer of 1839 when he had his first serious doubts about the Anglican position. Newman's own free translation of these 'palmary

---

[104] *Dev.* 189, 195–6.   [105] *Dev.* 199–200, 203.   [106] *Dev.* 203.

words' of Augustine was: 'The universal Church is in its judgments secure of truth.'[107]

Judged, then, by Newman's tests or notes *Dignitatis Humanae* is an authentic doctrinal development. And, in the face of the rejection by the Lefebvrists of the document, Newman's seven 'tests' or 'notes' do very usefully 'serve as answers to objections brought against the...decisions of authority.'[108] However, they also answer those on the opposite wing of the Church who hold also that the document constitutes a rupture with past teaching, albeit in their view a welcome rupture. Thus, in his book *A Church that Can and Cannot Change*, John T. Noonan Jr. asks how can what he calls the 'old message of intolerance, massively delivered over fifteen hundred years...be swept away by one pope and council?' He correctly points out that 'Vatican II itself did not attempt to grapple with this question. *Dignitatis humanae personae* did not mention the teaching of the past.' The fact that the document admitted 'mistakes' in the past 'was not the same as explaining how the Church could teach one thing in the past, another thing today'. In Noonan's view, the 'dilemma' for the Council 'seemed inescapable: Admit it, you were wrong then, or you are wrong now.' And he adds that this change in teaching raised another question: 'if fifteen hundred years of doctrine could be cancelled by one council and pope, why could the new teaching not be trumped in turn?'[109]

In his review of Noonan's book, Cardinal Avery Dulles points out first that Noonan ignores the essentially different social conditions in which the Church had formerly dealt with the question of religious freedom.

Far from the kind of pluralist society we have become accustomed to in the West, Christian Europe in the past was a society in which Religion provided the moral and cultural framework in which the society functioned. The state professed a particular religion and expected the citizens to adhere to it, while making exceptions for certain minorities who were treated with varying degrees of tolerance. An attack upon the established religion was counted as a civil offense. And so, for most of

---

[107] *Apologia pro Vita Sua*, ed. Ian Ker (London: Penguin, 1994), 115; *Ess.* ii.101.
[108] *Dev.* 78.
[109] John T. Noonan, Jr., *A Church that Can and Cannot Change: The Development of Catholic Moral Teaching* (Notre Dame, IN: University of Notre Dame Press, 2005), 157–8.

its history, Christianity functioned within a social system in which civil authorities upheld the religion of the people. The expectation was that the state would support the true religion. The Second Vatican Council still teaches...that it is legitimate for the constitutional order of society to give special recognition to one religious body such as the Catholic Church.

There is another factor that needs to be taken into consideration. In the nineteenth century secular liberals argued that freedom of conscience meant that the state should not concern itself with religion. Religion should be a private matter in a purely secular society. This separation of Church and state led to anti-clerical persecution of the Church as a body in society. That was the context of papal condemnations of religious freedom in the nineteenth century, not the kind of separation of Church and state as understood in the United States. As for the Second Vatican Council, Dulles points out, the Declaration on Religious Freedom explicitly 'leaves intact the traditional Catholic teaching on the moral duty of individuals and societies towards the true religion and the one Church of Christ' (art. 1). Thus, paradoxically, Noonan put himself in the same position as Archbishop Lefebvre in regarding *Dignitatis Humanae* as a departure from the tradition of the Church. John Courtney Murray, on the contrary, was quite clear that it was an authentic doctrinal development. And Dulles concludes that the Council 'applied the unchanging principles of the right to religious freedom and the duty to uphold religious truth to the conditions of an individualist age, in which almost all societies are religiously pluralist. Under such circumstances the establishment of religion becomes the exception rather than the rule. But the principle of noncoercion of consciences in matters of faith remains constant.'[110]

---

[110] Avery Cardinal Dulles, SJ, 'Development or Reversal?' *First Things* (October 2005), 53–61.

3

Towards a Theology of Councils

1

In the first chapter we looked at Newman's consistency during both his Anglican and Catholic years in resisting liberalism while at the same time remaining open to radical new ideas. While insisting on continuity, he did not see change as necessarily a rupture with tradition. In the second chapter we considered, firstly, the correctness or truthfulness of Newman's account of his religious history in his *Apologia pro Vita Sua*; secondly, we tested whether this history could be shown to represent authentic development, that is change but change in continuity, in terms of his own seven tests or notes; and, thirdly, we tested in the same way the most controversial of the documents of Vatican II to see whether it evinced rupture or continuity with the tradition. In this chapter we will look at Newman's reflections on Church Councils, on how they represent both change and continuity, to see if they might provide a hermeneutic to help us understand better the meaning and significance of the Second Vatican Council, as well as the implications for the post-conciliar Church.

In August 1831, when Newman wrote to tell H.J. Rose that the history of Councils that he had been asked to contribute to the new theological library would have to be in two volumes, he added that what was needed was 'a *connected* history of the Councils...not taking them as isolated, but introducing so much of Church History as will illustrate and account for them'. The remark is significant for two reasons. First, it shows that Newman was above all a *historical* theologian, who was convinced that theology should not be separated from history: 'What light would be thrown on the Nicene Confession *merely* by explaining it article by article? To understand it, it must be prefaced by a sketch of the rise of the Arian heresy…'. This didn't mean that Newman *identified* the theologian with the historical theologian: he was not envisaging always 'combining history and doctrinal discussion'.[1] But equally, just as it was impossible to isolate theology from history, so too it was not possible to study Church history independently of theology. And Newman made no bones about the fact that he would be writing his history in the context of his opposition to contemporary theological liberalism: he would inevitably be 'resisting the innovations of the day, and attempting to defend the work of men indefinitely above me (the Primitive Fathers) which is now assailed'.[2] Second, the remark anticipates the way in which Newman was to become acutely aware of the interdependence of Councils that could only be properly understood in relation to each other.

On 26 June 1867 Pope Pius IX announced that a General Council was to be convened. The prospect of the definition of papal infallibility particularly concerned Newman, not just because of the doctrine but because all dogmatic definitions by Councils were bound to stir up controversy. Even in the case of the early Councils, which had been necessary because of heresies, there had been a great deal of confusion and dissension in the wake of their decisions. In the case of papal infallibility there were none of those 'heretical questionings' that, Newman had pointed out in the *Apologia*, 'have been transmuted by the living power of the Church into salutary truths'.[3] Even at this early stage Newman was well aware that Councils can have effects that are *not* intended. If the Council were to define the doctrine of papal infallibility, there would be wide repercussions. A definition would necessarily lead to 'an alteration of the *elementary constitution* of the Church' in so far as it would encourage popes to act independently of the bishops.[4]

Quite apart from the danger of the kind of extreme definition that the Ultramontane party would be pressing for, Newman objected, as we have seen,[5] to the opportuneness of any definition, however moderate: 'We do not move at railroad pace in theological matters, even in the 19th century.' It was particularly serious if 'a grave dogmatic question was being treated merely as a move in ecclesiastical politics'.[6]

But although Newman was scandalized by the intrigues of the Ultramontanes, he could not agree with the German Church historian

---

[1] *LD* ii.352–3.   [2] *LD* iii.43.   [3] *Apo.* 237.   [4] *LD* xxiv.377.
[5] See Chapter 1, section 5, p. 33.   [6] *LD* xxv.93, 95.

Johann Döllinger that their behaviour in any way affected the valid-
ity of the Council. Such political manoeuvring was unfortunately a
feature of Councils, for they had 'ever been times of great *trial*' and
'the conduct of individuals who composed them was no measure of
their result.'[7] History showed that Councils had 'generally two characteristics—a great deal of violence and intrigue on the part of the
actors in them, and a great resistance to their definitions on the part
of portions of Christendom.'[8]

Although the wording of the definition that was eventually passed
was weaker than what the Ultramontanes had wanted and was quite
acceptable in theory to Newman, still in practice, 'considered in its
effects both upon the Pope's mind and that of his people, it is nothing else than shooting Niagara'. Nevertheless, however scandalous the
proceedings at the Council, that was no excuse for Döllinger and other
liberal Catholics to exaggerate what had actually been defined. The
important thing, Newman urged in his private correspondence, was
patience: 'Remedies spring up naturally in the Church, as in nature,
if we wait for them.' The definition could not simply be considered by
itself: the context, or rather lack of context, was very important, for
'the definition was taken out of its order—it would have come to us
very differently, if those preliminaries about the Church's power had
first been passed, which...were intended'.[9] If the Council, which had
been cut short prematurely by political events and suspended indefinitely by the Pope, did reassemble, it would hopefully 'occupy itself in
other points' which would 'have the effect of qualifying and guarding
the dogma'.[10] If this was not to be, then the Council would be modified
and completed by another Council, as had happened before in the
history of the Church. Characteristically, Newman turned for guidance to the history of the early Church:

> Another consideration has struck me forcibly, and that is, that, look-
> ing at early history, it would seem as if the Church moved on to the
> perfect truth by various successive declarations, alternately in contrary
> directions, and thus perfecting, completing, supplying each other. Let
> us have a little faith in her, I say. Pius is not the last of the Popes—the
> fourth Council modified the third, the fifth the fourth...The late defini-
> tion does not so much need to be undone, as to be completed. It needs
> *safeguards* to the Pope's possible acts—explanations as to the matter and

---

[7] *LD* xxv.158.   [8] *LD* xxvi.281.   [9] *LD* xxv.262.
[10] *LD* xxv.278.

extent of his power. I know that a violent reckless party, had it its will, would at this moment define that the Pope's powers need no safeguards, no explanations—but there is a limit to the triumph of the tyrannical— Let us be patient, let us have faith, and a new Pope, and a re-assembled Council may trim the boat.[11]

2

This is a remarkable prophecy of the Second Vatican Council. And it is particularly remarkable when one considers that after the First Vatican Council it was widely believed that there would be no need of future Councils, and that Newman himself had acknowledged that Councils might be interfered with by governments putting pressure on weak bishops and that an infallible papacy would be more effective in putting paid to the kind of controversies out of which heresies arose.[12]

Newman's point about the Church moving 'alternately in contrary directions' obviously applies to the Second Vatican Council which was hardly a linear continuation of the First Vatican Council. If Newman is correct, the hope expressed by liberal Catholics that there will be another Council that will be a kind of continuation of Vatican II is historically unrealistic.

The early Councils showed how doctrines 'were not struck off all at once but piecemeal—one Council did one thing, another a second— and so the whole dogma was built up'. It was because 'the first portion of it looked extreme' that controversies arose which led to subsequent Councils that '*explained* and *completed* what was first done'.[13] In the case of Vatican I the definition of papal infallibility needed explaining and completing by the teaching of Vatican II on the pope as the head—but also therefore a member—of the college of bishops.

Again, the history of the early Church showed how Councils led to confusion and dissension. So much was this the case after Vatican I that Newman could even write: 'We do not know what exactly we hold—what we may grant, what we must maintain.' Theologians, he pointed out, had had three hundred years to explain and interpret the

---

[11] *LD* xxv.310.   [12] See Chapter 1, section 5, p. 34.
[13] *LD* xxv.330.

Council of Trent—but 'now we are new born children, the birth of the Vatican Council'.[14] Councils, he explained, 'generally acted as a lever, displacing and disordering portions of the existing theological system' and leading to acrimonious controversy.[15] These words are a very apt description of what happened after the Second Vatican Council, for, even though it may have defined no dogma, the chaos and upheaval that followed the effective closure of the era of the Tridentine Church far exceeded that of the First Vatican Council, which had practically no effect on the ordinary Catholic.

Having been an 'inopportunist' or opponent of a definition of papal infallibility before the Council, ironically Newman came to far prefer the papacy to Councils, which were, 'with a few exceptions, a dreary, unlovely phenomenon in the Church': 'The more one examines the Councils, the less satisfactory they are—the less satisfactory they, the more majestic and trust-winning, and the more imperatively necessary, is the action of the Holy See.'[16]

But the proceedings and decisions of Councils were one thing, the interpretation of their teachings another thing. As Newman had pointed out before the definition of papal infallibility, the definition, if there was one, would require explanation and interpretation, and the same would be true of any definitions made in future by a pope. Just as 'lawyers explain acts of Parliament', so theologians explain the teachings of the Church: 'Hence, I have never been able to see myself that the ultimate decision rest with any but the general Catholic intelligence.'[17] For not only are theologians involved, 'the voice of the Schola Theologorum', but 'the whole Church diffusive' would ultimately 'assimilate and harmonize' the definition within the whole context of Catholic belief.[18] It was, however, the special task of theologians to 'settle the force of the wording of the dogma, just as the courts of law solve the meaning and bearing of Acts of Parliament'.[19] For the meaning of 'dogmatic statements' was not self-evident, but they were 'always made with the anticipation and condition of this lawyer-like, or special-pleader-like action, of the intellect upon them'.[20] Popes and Councils possessed an 'active infallibility', but what Newman called a *passive infallibility* belonged to 'the whole body of

---

[14] *LD* xxvi.59–60.   [15] *LD* xxvi.76.   [16] *LD* xxvi.120; xxviii.172.
[17] *LD* xxv.71.   [18] *LD* xxv.284.   [19] *LD* xxv.447.
[20] *LD* xxvi.35.

the Catholic people' who 'determine the general sense of authoritative words', while the theologians have the responsibility for distinguishing between 'theological truth and theological opinion'.[21] He by no means ruled out the possibility of 'a false interpretation' of the definition. And in so far as there developed after the Council the phenomenon called 'creeping infallibility', and in so far as bishops came to be seen as merely delegates of the pope, then Newman's prophecy that 'another Leo will be given for the occasion' proved to be true. Pope St Leo's Council of Chalcedon, 'without of course touching the definition' of the preceding Council of Ephesus, had 'trimmed the balance of doctrine by completing it'.[22] Similarly, Blessed Pope John xxiii called the Second Vatican Council which, in its Constitution on the Church, 'trimmed the balance of doctrine by completing' the First Vatican Council's teaching on the papacy with a much fuller teaching on the Church.

3

The controversies and dissensions that followed in the wake of Vatican ii would hardly have surprised Newman. One of the 'disadvantages of a General Council', he knew, 'is that it throws individual units through the Church into confusion and sets them at variance'. There was nothing surprising about the emergence of the Old Catholic Church after Vatican i, nor about the exaggerations of the definition of papal infallibility by the extreme Ultramontanes. Similarly, Newman would hardly have been surprised either by the Lefebvrist schism after Vatican ii or by the extremism of the progressive faction led by the Swiss theologian Hans Küng. In the aftermaths of both Councils it suited the extreme protagonists on both wings of the Church so to exaggerate what the Councils had taught as to make them seem like revolutionary events, cutting the Church off from its past. In Newman's view, as we have seen,[23] Döllinger's appeal to history against the definition was like using 'private judgment' to interpret 'Scripture against the voice of authority'; but if the latter was 'unlawful', why should it 'be lawful

---

[21] *LD* xxvii.338.   [22] *Diff.* ii.312.
[23] See Chapter 1, section ii.5, pp. 36–7.

in the interpretation of history'? What was important was 'faith in the word of the Church'. At the other end of the spectrum was Cardinal Manning of Westminster, who, in Newman's view, had used extraordinary 'rhetoric', particularly in his pastoral letter of October 1870, which gave the impression that papal infallibility was unlimited in its scope.[24] Newman would surely have been at least as critical of Hans Küng and so-called 'progressive Catholics' who, just as the extreme Ultramontanes did their best to encourage 'creeping infallibility', regularly appeal to 'the spirit of Vatican II' in order to advance an agenda for which there is no warrant in the text of the documents of that Council. On the other hand, just as he had condemned Döllinger and his followers for appealing to history against the Church, so too Newman would have rejected the Lefebvrists' appeal to tradition against the teachings of Vatican II.

In Newman's reflections on Councils and their aftermaths, two different kinds of development are involved. One kind is illustrated by one of his most illuminating images. In the first section of the first chapter of *An Essay on the Development of Christian Doctrine*, Newman, speaking about the process of development of ideas, points out that a living idea cannot be isolated 'from intercourse with the world around'. Far from this being a danger, he argues that this contact is actually necessary 'if a great idea is duly to be understood, and much more if it is to be fully exhibited'.

Although he concedes that there is always the risk of an 'idea' being corrupted by external elements, Newman nevertheless insists that, while 'It is indeed sometimes said that the stream is clearest near the spring', this is not true of the kind of philosophical or religious 'idea' that he has in mind:

> Whatever use may fairly be made of this image, it does not apply to the history of a philosophy or belief, which on the contrary is more equable, and purer, and stronger, when its bed has become deep, and broad, and full. It necessarily rises out of an existing state of things, and for a time savours of the soil. Its vital element needs disengaging from what is foreign and temporary…[25]

It is worth noting that the conclusion to this section contains one of the best known of Newman quotations, but since it is invariably quoted out of context, it is invariably misinterpreted. The famous

---

[24] *LD* xxvii.383; xxv.230.   [25] *Dev.* 39–40.

words are: 'In a higher world it is otherwise, but here below to live is to change, and to be perfect is to have changed often.' This is regularly taken as a slogan for a progressivist agenda of change, change that is in clear rupture with the past. But what Newman has in mind is change *in continuity with the past*. For the sentence that precedes the famous words and which is never quoted makes clear the kind of change that is envisaged: 'It [a philosophical or religious "idea"] changes with them [external circumstances] in order to remain the same.'[26]

Now, if Newman is correct that an 'idea' such as a philosophy or a belief becomes 'more equable, and purer, and stronger' as it changes, that is, develops because it remains the same, then this is a principle which we can plausibly apply to the 'idea' of the Second Vatican Council. The participants in and observers of the Council no doubt thought they knew very well what, for better or worse, the Council meant and signified. Both Lefebvre and Küng had no doubt as to how the Council was to be understood, and of course paradoxically, like Döllinger and Manning, were in close agreement about its meaning and significance: for both it was a revolutionary event signalling a rupture with the past and tradition. However, just as in retrospect and with a better historical perspective we can appreciate much better than Döllinger and Manning the strict limitations of Vatican I's definition of papal infallibility, so too we are surely in a better position, as the dust, so to speak, has gradually settled, to understand Vatican II as a Council of reform not revolution, of reform in continuity with the tradition. Now if it is true that Newman is rightly called 'the Father of the Second Vatican Council', then it seems not unreasonable to use the mini-theology of Councils that he adumbrated at the time of the First Vatican Council, in conjunction with his theory of development, as a hermeneutic for Vatican II. As has been well said, while before the Council Newman was 'still an occasionally suspect stranger, an outsider to the neo-scholastic' world of Catholic theology, after the Council he became 'its godfather and our guide into the strange territory that now lay before us'.[27]

Vatican II did not take place in a historical void; it met in a decade of enormous upheaval, a time of optimistic euphoria, as well as a moral

---

[26] *Dev.* 40.
[27] Nicholas Lash, 'Tides and Twilight: Newman since Vatican II', in Ian Ker and Alan G. Hill, eds, *Newman after a Hundred Years* (Oxford: Clarendon Press, 1990), 454.

and social revolution in the Western world. Inevitably, the Council 'savoured' of 'the soil' of the 1960s, of the 'existing state of things'. If Newman is right, then we should expect the 'idea' of Vatican II to grow 'more equable, and purer, and stronger' as the 'stream' moves away from the 'spring' and 'its bed has become deep, and broad, and full', for its 'vital element needs disengaging from what is foreign and temporary'. And it is not irrelevant to note how often after Vatican I Newman reiterated that time is the great healer: 'our duty is patience'. There was, it is true, a wait of nearly a hundred years, but patience had its reward in 1962 with the opening of the Second Vatican Council. 'Our wisdom is to keep quiet,' Newman wrote in a private letter of 1871, 'not to make controversy, not to make things worse, but to pray that He, who before now has completed a first Council by a second, may do so now.'[28]

The other kind of development is referred to by Newman in that mini-theology of Councils that he sketched out in his private letters at the time of Vatican I. For it is not only a question of the meaning and significance of an 'idea' like the theology of Vatican II becoming more luminous and focused as it is seen in retrospect and from a historical perspective, but there is also the consideration that Councils open up further developments because of what they do *not* say or stress, what they fail to teach or define: thus Nicaea calls for Ephesus and Vatican I for Vatican II. Neither Ephesus nor Vatican II requires that kind of completion by another Council. In any case, Vatican II completed its business, whereas Vatican I had to be suspended and never reassembled, having met for less than a year.

Newman's prediction, then, that the incomplete ecclesiology of Vatican I needed to be completed by another Council was a well-founded historical prediction. Vatican II, however, does not obviously call for any such completion. It is true that there are those on the liberal wing of the Catholic Church who would like to see a Third Vatican Council which would be simply a kind of continuation of the Second Vatican Council. But that is to ignore the fact that history does not stand still: new problems, new priorities arise. And on the new challenge that the Church faced in a rapidly secularizing world the Council had nothing specifically to say.

---

[28] *LD* xxv.278.

For, apart from the Decree on the Church's Missionary Activity (*Ad Gentes*), the Second Vatican Council was silent on the subject of evangelization. Not only was there no document devoted to the topic, but it was not even the subject of a section, let alone chapter, in the Pastoral Constitution on the Church in the Modern World (*Gaudium et Spes*), where it could only be said to surface on occasion as a theme by implication. And so in 1975, ten years after the Council, Pope Paul VI issued *Evangelii Nuntiandi*, thus re-directing the attention of a Church that had become preoccupied with internal reforms and relations with other churches and other religions and the world to the original mandate given to it by Christ—'Go, therefore, make disciples of all the nations' (Mt. 28:19).

And this brings us to the most striking phenomenon in the post-conciliar Church, the spectacular rise of the new ecclesial movements and communities, some of which actually pre-date the Council. Significantly, these movements and communities are not only of great importance for evangelization, but they also illuminate by realizing in the concrete one of the two most important texts of Vatican II. As Pope Paul VI pointed out in his first encyclical (1964), *Ecclesiam Suam*, the Church was 'the principal object of attention' (art. 33) of Vatican II.[29] And clearly from a strictly dogmatic point of view, the third and longest chapter of the Constitution on the Church (*Lumen Gentium*) on the hierarchy was the most important text as it balanced, modified, and completed Vatican I's definition of papal infallibility with its teaching on the relationship between the papacy and the episcopate. But from the point of view of the renewal of the Church and of the new evangelization, the most important text is, I would argue, the first and especially the second chapters where the Council seeks to describe the fundamental nature of the Church.

But these two chapters attracted little or no attention after the Council—except in so far as Chapter 2, 'The People of God', was mistakenly taken to *be* a chapter on the laity—when the chapter that seemed most important apart from the one on the hierarchy was the fourth chapter on the laity. However, the contrast between the ecclesiology of the former and the latter is very striking. Whereas the first two chapters are thoroughly scriptural and patristic, the fourth

---

[29]   Avery Dulles, SJ, 'The Church', in Walter M. Abbot, SJ, ed., *The Documents of Vatican II* (London: Geoffrey Chapman, 1966), 12.

chapter is unable to cite a single New Testament source, where of course both the word and concept are unknown. There is only one reference to the Fathers, a famous quotation from St Augustine: 'To you I am the bishop, with you I am a Christian' (art. 31). The word 'lay' is not mentioned, and the quotation really is consistent with the ecclesiology of Chapter 2 not Chapter 4, which presupposes a Church divided into clergy and laity. But in Chapter 2, which is called 'The People of God', the Church is described as an organic communion of those who 'are reborn...from water and the Holy Spirit' in baptism (art. 9). The baptized constitute 'a holy priesthood, although this 'common priesthood of the faithful' differs 'essentially and not only in degree' from 'the ministerial or hierarchical priesthood' (art. 10). This 'priestly community is brought into operation through the sacraments'. First, there are the sacraments of initiation—baptism, confirmation, and Eucharist—which all the members of the people of God are expected to receive; then there are the sacraments of penance and anointing, which again the faithful should normally receive at some point or points in their lives; and finally, two sacraments which not all members of the people of God receive—holy orders and marriage (art. 11). The people of God are certainly not just the laity—as is practically assumed by the 'proponents of democratization' of the Church who conclude that this gives 'priority to the laity and leaves the hierarchy in a secondary role as servants'[30]—but 'the whole people... "from the bishops to the last of the faithful"' (art. 12). The chapter carefully avoids talking of the Church in terms of the clergy and the laity. For this is the Church of St Paul: 'Now you together are Christ's body; but each of you is a different part of it. In the Church, God has given the first place to apostles, the second to prophets, the third to teachers; after them, miracles, and after them the gift of healing; helpers, good leaders, those with many languages' (1 Cor. 12:27–8).

Now the ecclesial movements and communities are not infrequently referred to as lay movements and communities—which is exactly what they are not, for, although obviously the majority of the

---

[30]   Avery Cardinal Dulles, SJ, 'Nature, Mission, and Structure of the Church', in Matthew L. Lamb and Matthew Levering, eds, *Vatican II: Renewal within Tradition* (New York: Oxford University Press, 2008), 31. Cf. Aidan Nichols, OP, *The Thought of Pope Benedict XVI: An Introduction to the Theology of Joseph Ratzinger* (London and New York: Burns & Oates, 2007), 177: 'the formula "People of God" is in danger of becoming a vehicle for an anti-hierarchical ecclesiology, a revolutionary category in which to appropriate the concept of a "new" Church'.

members are lay, they are open to the whole people of God, whether clergy, religious, or laity, some of them even having their own priests and consecrated members. In other words, they are truly *ecclesial*.[31] The Church of Chapter 2 of *Lumen Gentium* is thus concretely realized in microcosm in these ecclesial movements and communities, and the notional 'idea' of the Church as the organic communion of the baptized becomes a living reality. The significance of this revolutionary chapter, revolutionary because it 'rolled' the Church back to the ecclesiology of the New Testament and the Fathers, was obscured at the time of the Council and in the years after, when the chapters on the bishops and laity were at the centre of attention because of the need to modify in the sense of balancing the papal infallibility definition and the need to stress the importance of the laity in what had become a highly clericalized Church. It was in the context of that 'existing state of things' that Chapter 2 was hardly noticed. But, as Newman noted, 'the stream' is not 'clearest near the spring' in the case of the history of a philosophical or religious idea, and during the half-century that has passed since the end of the Second Vatican Council, with the astronomic growth of the new movements and communities and their growing importance in the Church, in striking contrast to the dramatic decline of the active religious orders, in particular the Jesuits, the great order of the Counter-Reformation, the theology of Chapter 2 has become much clearer in its prophetic significance: 'its bed has become deep, and broad, and full'.[32]

---

[31] See Chapter 4, section 5, p. 105.   [32] *Dev.* 40.

4

The Charismatic Church

1

As we have seen, the major theological item on the Second Vatican Council's agenda was the question of the relationship of the episcopate to the papacy, given the definition of papal infallibility at the First Vatican Council and that Council's failure to provide a larger teaching about the Church. 'Continuing in the . . . task of clarification begun by Vatican I', Vatican II's Constitution on the Church teaches that Christ 'formed' the Apostles 'after the manner of a college, over which He placed Peter'.[1] This so-called doctrine of collegiality has been a bone of contention since the Council, for it places the pope within this 'apostolic college' and yet also above it, since the Council also teaches that the pope possesses 'power of primacy over all, pastors as well as the general faithful'.[2] Since the Council, the popes have appointed diocesan bishops to senior posts within the Roman Curia, as well as convening regular international synods of bishops. In 2013 Pope Francis appointed eight cardinals from around the world to advise him on the government of the Church and the reform of the Roman Curia,[3] as well as calling for an enhanced status for Episcopal conferences in the same year.[4] But such reforms will never satisfy the ultra-liberal wing of the Church which sees papal 'power of primacy' as contrary to authentic episcopal collegiality and to 'the spirit of Vatican II' and looks forward to a Vatican III that will make it clear that the pope is

---

[1] *Lumen Gentium*, 18, 19.   [2] *Lumen Gentium*, 22.
[3] <http://www.zenit.org/en/articles/pope-appoints-group-of-cardinals-to-advise-on-church-governance>
[4] Apostolic Exhortation, *Evangelli Gaudium*, art. 32.

merely 'primus inter pares', first among equals, simply the chairman of the college of bishops, a kind of glorified Archbishop of Canterbury.

Ironically, having been an inopportunist, Newman became, as we have seen, more papal and less conciliar in his ecclesiology after the definition of papal infallibility, disgusted as he was by the intrigues and manoeuvring behind the scenes at Vatican I. Increased papal authority, he believed, would at least put an end to the idea of national churches such as the Gallican Church.[5] He would certainly have been dismayed by the way in the immediate aftermath of Vatican II certain episcopal conferences seemed to be moving in the direction of creating quasi-national churches in communion with but in impaired union with the papacy.

It is true that Newman in his day deplored the excessive power of the Congregation de Propaganda Fide, the missionary department of the Roman Curia: 'the whole English-speaking Catholic population all over the world is under Propaganda, an arbitrary, military power...And who *is* Propaganda? one sharp man of business, who...dispatches his work quick off, to the East and the West, a high dignitary...but after all little more than a clerk, or (according to his name) a Secretary, with two or three clerks under him.'[6] But, although Newman condemned this 'extreme centralization',[7] any concept of a national church was repugnant to him. One of the reasons why, in spite of his having been so heavily influenced by the Eastern rather than the Western Fathers, he would never have contemplated becoming an Orthodox was what he called its deplorable 'consecration of the principle of nationalism' in the form of ethnic churches.[8]

2

The third chapter of the Constitution on the Church on the episcopate may be the most important dogmatic text of the Second Vatican Council in so far as it completes the unfinished business of the First Vatican Council, but it is not, I have suggested, the most important

---

[5] See Chapter 1, section II.5, p. 34.   [6] *LD* xx.391.
[7] *LD* xx.391, 447.
[8] *HS* i.203. See Ian Ker, *Newman and the Fullness of Christianity* (Edinburgh: T & T Clark, 1993), 100–2.

text of the Council so far as the renewal of the Church and evangelization are concerned—and, I might add, the cause of Christian unity. The most important and seminal texts, from these points of view, are, in my view, the first two chapters of the Constitution where the Council considers the fundamental nature of the Church by returning to the sources in the Scriptures and the Fathers, and defines the Church primarily not in hierarchical terms but as the communion of those who receive the gift of the Holy Spirit in baptism. But the other significant feature of these two chapters is the stress they place on the special gifts that the Holy Spirit bestows on the baptized.

This emphasis on the charismatic dimension of the Church has been largely unnoticed in the years since the Council. Indeed, in a very recent authoritative commentary on the first four chapters of *Lumen Gentium* by the distinguished ecclesiologist the late Cardinal Avery Dulles, there is a deafening silence on this charismatic dimension.[9] And yet in the first two chapters there are no less than three references to the charisms.[10] First, the Constitution says that the Holy Spirit bestows upon the Church 'varied hierarchic and charismatic gifts' (art. 4). Second, it makes a distinction of priority between these different gifts: 'Among these gifts the primacy belongs to the grace of the apostles to whose authority the Spirit Himself subjects even those who are endowed with charisms' (art. 7). But third, at greater length, the constitution affirms the importance of the charisms:

> It is not only through the sacraments and the ministrations of the Church that the Holy Spirit makes holy the people, leads them and enriches them with his virtues. Allotting his gifts according as he wills (cf. 1 Cor. 12:11), he also distributes special graces among the faithful of every rank. By these gifts he makes them fit and ready to undertake various tasks and offices for the renewal and building up of the Church, as it is written, 'the manifestation of the Spirit is given to everyone for profit' (1. Cor. 12:7). Whether these charisms be very remarkable or more simple and widely diffused, they are to be received with thanksgiving and consolation since they are fitting and useful for the needs of the Church. (art. 12)

---

[9]   Avery Cardinal Dulles, SJ, 'Nature, Mission, and Structure of the Church', in Matthew L. Lamb and Matthew Levering, eds, *Vatican II: Renewal within Tradition* (New York: Oxford University Press, 2008), 25–36.

[10]   The following is largely an adapted and revised version of my 'Newman and the Charismatic Dimension of the Church', in Terrence Merrigan and Ian Ker, eds, *Newman and Truth* (Louvain: Peeters; Grand Rapids: Eerdmans, 2008), 251–80.

Commenting on this latter text, Pope John Paul II said that it was under the guidance of the Holy Spirit that the Council 'rediscovered the charismatic dimension as one of [the Church's] constitutive elements', and that the 'institutional and charismatic aspects are co-essential as it were to the Church's constitution'.[11] In his commentary on this text, published two years after the end of the Council, Aloys Grillmeier also notes that, as well as speaking of the work of the Spirit in sacraments and ministries, 'it is equally important that the Council says a special word about the "charisms", the special gifts of grace in the Church'. And he proceeds to quote from an article by Hans Küng, 'The Charismatic Structure of the Church', published in the journal *Concilium* in 1965, the same year the Council ended:

> The charismata are not primarily extraordinary but common; they are not of one kind, but manifold; they are not limited to a special group of persons, but truly universal in the Church. All this implies also that they are not a thing of the past (possible and real only in the early Church), but eminently contemporary and actual; they do not hover on the periphery of the Church but are eminently central and essential to it. In this sense one should speak of a *charismatic structure of the Church* which embraces and goes beyond the structure of its government.[12]

However, writing twenty-five years after the Council, in his article 'The Biblical Question of "Charisms" after Vatican II', Albert Vanhoye is sharply critical of what was taken in the immediate aftermath of the Council to be the authoritative explanation of what *Lumen Gentium* meant by charisms. He begins by pointing out that, while 'The concept of charisms has its starting point in certain New Testament texts that speak of *charisma*', nevertheless in Western theology 'the generalized use of the technical term "charism" is of relatively recent date', in view of the fact that the 'word is found only once in the Vulgate', whereas elsewhere the word is translated by several different words. When Latin theologians following St Thomas Aquinas want to speak of charism they use the phrase 'gratia gratis data'. With Vatican II, the vocabulary changes, since the official conciliar texts, written in Latin, use the Latin transliteration

---

[11] *Movements in the Church: Proceedings of the World Congress of the Ecclesial Movements, Rome, 27–29 May 1998* (Vatican City: Pontificium Consilium pro Laicis, 1999), 221.

[12] *Commentary on the Documents of Vatican II*, vol. 2, ed. Herbert Vorgrimler (London: Burns & Oates, 1967), 165.

of the Greek word, except in quotations from the New Testament where the Vulgate is used. At the Council itself, there was a clash between the conservatives who viewed charisms as extraordinary, miraculous gifts, and the reformers who successfully pressed for charisms to be seen as much more ordinary gifts belonging to baptized Christians, such as the gifts of catechesis and evangelization. It was this position that prevailed in *Lumen Gentium*.

However, Vanhoye regards the interpretation of charisms by Küng, which he reproduced in his book *The Church* (1967), as unfaithful to the concilar texts on charisms and overdependent on the influential study 'Ministry and Community' (1964) by the Protestant theologian E. Käsemann. Thus Küng uncritically accepts the concept of charism as describing all ecclesial services and functions. Vanhoye argues that Küng so broadens the notion of charism as to rob it of any 'identifying characteristic'. For example, Küng sees Christian love as the highest as well as the most ordinary of the charisms. But Vanhoye points out that this is only possible if we take charism to mean simply a gift as opposed to 'a special grace granted to one Christian and not to another'. But it is manifest that when Vatican II rediscovered what Pope John Paul II called the charismatic dimension, it was doing something more significant than saying that all the Christian virtues are gifts. If that was all that *Lumen Gentium* intended in those three texts in the first two chapters, then the dispute between the reformers and the conservatives was pointless, as both sides would have agreed that the Christian virtues are gifts. But the issue was whether or not ordinary Christians can possess special charisms which help to build up the Church, or whether the Church is to be seen as sustained primarily and for the most part (except in extraordinary and miraculous instances) by the ministry and sacraments of the ordained priesthood. But, as Vanhoye sarcastically puts it, 'meekly' following the Protestant Käsemann, Küng sees charisms everywhere, and so evacuates the term of any special meaning that 'it loses any substance and it becomes difficult to see how the charisms could then provide the Church with a "structure"'.

Of course, Küng has a very definite agenda in extending the sense of charism, and that is, to quote Vanhoye again, his anxiety 'to limit the sphere of responsibility of the pastors of the Church as much as possible'. Insistent that charisms are not the preserve of the hierarchy, 'he describes everything as a charism, from theological charity to the actions of eating and drinking. In this way, the authorities of the Church are, so to speak, drowned in an ocean of charisms possessed by all the members of the faithful.' But then Küng introduces another concept of charisms as the personal gifts belonging to individuals called to a particular ministry within the Church. This is the basis for his idea of a 'charismatic structure' of the Church, which is very different from saying that the Church has a charismatic dimension. But the Church also has a hierarchical dimension, indeed structure, which, according to *Lumen Gentium*, discerns and regulates the charismatic dimension: 'Those who have charge over the Church should judge the genuineness and proper use of these gifts, through their office not indeed to extinguish the Spirit, but to test all things and hold fast to what is good' (art. 12). This specific teaching of the Council is ignored by Küng, unsurprisingly. To the question as to how unity is to be preserved in the kind of charismatic Church that Küng envisages, he replies that the same Spirit who gives the charisms also creates unity and order. This is certainly true, but the Spirit acts through the hierarchical dimension, as St Paul says in 1 Corinthians: 'In the Church, God has given the first place to apostles, the second to prophets, the third to teachers; after them, miracles, and after them the gift of healing; helpers, good leaders, those with many languages' (12:28).

These are precisely the 'varied hierarchic and charismatic gifts' of *Lumen Gentium*, where the hierarchical also takes precedence. Paul himself gives concrete examples of ways in which apostolic authority is to be exercised with regard to the charisms, and adds that what he writes 'is a command from the Lord' (1 Cor. 14: 27–9, 37). As a Biblical exegete himself, Vanhoye concludes that, while in the New Testament the Greek word *charisma* often has only too general or too specific meaning of gift to be translated by the word charism, nevertheless there are clear instances of *charisma* being used to describe a special gift given to an individual for the good of the Church, and it is this usage which the Council employs, 'following a theological tradition'.[13]

---

[13] Albert Vanhoye, SJ, 'The Biblical Question of "Charisms" after Vatican II', in *Vatican II: Assessment and Perspectives: Twenty-five Years After (1962–1987)*, vol. 1, ed. René Latourelle (Mahwah, NJ: Paulist Press, 1988), 439–68.

3

Turning now to Newman, we can certainly say that he, unlike Küng, is faithful to Scripture and tradition and in agreement with the Council that there is a charismatic dimension to the Church which involves more than just ordinary spiritual gifts and which is regulated by the hierarchical dimension. Naturally, Newman does not use the word charism because as we have seen the usage was not normal before the Council.

Newman found in the Fathers, who were bishops as well as charismatic figures, a union of the charismatic and hierarchical dimensions, a conjunction that was to be comparatively rare in succeeding centuries. His first written, as opposed to published, contribution to the Oxford Movement in 1833 was a paper which he intended to be 'one of a series' for the *British Magazine*, 'called the "Church of the Fathers"…on the principle of popularity as an element of Church power, as exemplified in the history of St Ambrose'. Far from being clerical, the early Church, in Newman's vivid phrase, 'threw itself on the *people*'.[14] And it is a very charismatic Church, in which there is a distinct place for prophets, for example: 'a child's voice, as is reported, was heard in the midst of the crowd to say, "Ambrose is bishop." '[15] At the time Ambrose was governor of the province and had been called to quell a disturbance in the cathedral in Milan, where the people had met to elect a new bishop. But Ambrose was not only not in holy orders but he was still only a catechumen awaiting baptism. However, on the prophetic word of a child he was unanimously elected bishop. So here we have a remarkable instance of charism preceding, so to speak, hierarchy.

The point of writing these sketches of the Church of the Fathers was to show how different the religion of the first centuries was from both Protestantism and the established Church of England. And one point Newman especially enjoys making is that if, as Protestants say, monasticism is a corruption of Christianity, then certainly Protestantism is a very different religion from early Christianity, for 'Could' a Protestant's 'present system…by any possibility be corrupted…into monasticism? Is there any sort of tendency in it towards—rather, are not all its tendencies from—such a result? If so, it

---

[14] *LD* iv.14, 18.   [15] *HS* i.343.

is plain that the religious temper of times is not like that of the primitive Church...'. In other words, Newman is arguing that the monastic charism—monasticism being the first great charismatic movement in the life of the Church—is the fruit of Catholic Christianity. It is not, however, as though non-Catholic Christians do not need or cannot be given charisms by the Spirit. They too can find themselves in a similar situation to the early Christians. 'One great purpose answered by Monasticism in the early ages was the maintenance of the Truth in times and places in which great masses of Catholics had let it slip from them.' Monasteries, Newman maintains,

> were intended as the refuge of piety and holiness, when the increasing spread of religion made Christians more secular. And we may confidently pronounce that such provisions, in one shape or other, will always be attempted by the more serious and anxious part of the community, whenever Christianity is generally professed. In Protestant countries, where monastic orders are unknown, men run into separatism with this object. Methodism has carried off many a man who was sincerely attached to the Established Church, merely because that Church will admit nothing but what it considers 'rational' and 'sensible' in religion.

If we may put it in a different way, where Christianity ceases to have a charismatic dimension, then what Newman would have called 'enthusiasm' finds no outlet within the Church. Because the charism of Wesley could find no place in the Church of England, he was led into schism from the hierarchical Church. Interestingly, Newman then goes on to point out, with remarkable vehemence, that the charism of religious life can provide much-needed community and support, especially for women in a society where they were denied opportunities:

> Convents are as much demanded, in the model of a perfect Church, by Christian charity, as monastic bodies can be by Christian zeal. I know not any more distressing development of the cruel temper of Protestantism than the determined, bitter, and scoffing spirit in which it has set itself against institutions which give dignity and independence to the position of women in society. As matters stand, marriage is almost the only shelter which a defenceless portion of the community has against the rude world;—a maiden life, that holy estate is not only left in desolateness, but oppressed with heartless ridicule and insult;— whereas, foundations for single women, under proper precautions, at once hold out protection to those who avail themselves of them and give dignity to the single state itself, and thus save numbers from the

temptation of throwing themselves rashly away upon unworthy objects, thereby transgressing their own sense of propriety, and embittering their future life.[16]

Newman's point can easily be applied to our own situation where an increasingly atomized and individualistic society, afflicted by the breakdown of marriage and family life, leads to much isolation and loneliness and loss of faith among Catholics whose needs the parish structure cannot meet but which can be met by the new ecclesial communities and movements. Newman's condemnation of those, not least in the hierarchical part of the Church, who dismiss or even forbid the new charisms which the Holy Spirit has provided for our situation and our times, and not least for the marginalized, would, I suspect, be no less severe than his strictures here on the Protestants of his day who rejected religious life out of hand. Those in the post-Vatican II Catholic Church who think that diocese and parish are quite sufficient for the needs of the people and any new movements of the Spirit are at best unnecessary and at worst divisive might reflect on what Newman as an Anglican has to say at the beginning of his biographical sketch of St Antony, where he castigates 'the tyranny of those who will not let a man do anything out of the way without stamping him with the name of fanatic'. This, Newman insists, the early Church did not do. Rather, it 'deals softly with the ardent and impetuous, saying, in effect—"... You wish to live above the common course of a Christian;—I can teach you to do this, yet without arrogance." '[17] In our own day this is exactly how Pope John Paul II spoke to the new ecclesial movements, whose members are often criticized for their arrogance, at a congress in 1998. Recalling how he had supported them from the beginning of his pontificate, he now recognized a greater maturity in them: 'Today I notice, with great joy, that [you] have a more mature self-knowledge.' On the other hand, the Pope seemed less sure that other parts of the Church, and of course he would have had in mind particularly the local episcopate and clergy, had grown similarly in knowledge of 'something new that is still waiting to be properly accepted and appreciated'. Or, as the then Cardinal Joseph Ratzinger put it more sharply, there is a danger of local bishops and churches turning 'their own pastoral plans into the criterion of what the Holy Spirit is allowed to do'.[18] Again, just

---

[16] *HS* ii.164–5.   [17] *HS* ii.96.   [18] *Movements in the Church*, 52–3.

as local Catholic bishops and clergy today are frequently opposed to the new movements entering their dioceses and parishes, so similarly Newman in the same passage deplored 'the sensible Protestant divine' who 'keeps to his point, hammering away on his own ideas, urging every one to be as every one else, and moulding all ideas upon his one small model; and when he has made his ground good to his own admiration, he finds that half his flock have after all turned Wesleyans or Independents, by way of searching for something divine and transcendental'.[19] One thinks today of the many Catholics in the United States and Latin America who have turned to Evangelical churches and sects, when their own Church has appeared more preoccupied with issues like social justice than with the gospel—that is, when the new movements have not been there to offer an alternative to what often appears a more secular than supernatural agenda.

In the early Church, on the other hand, where charism and hierarchy were in harmony and union with each other, 'enthusiasm' could flourish within the Church without getting out of control and without being suppressed. Thus St Antony, the founder of monasticism, would be called an 'enthusiast' in the Church of England of the 1830s, and would be

> exposed to a serious temptation of becoming a fanatic. Longing for some higher rule of life…and finding our present lines too rigidly drawn to include any character of mind that is much out of the way…he might possibly have broken what he could not bend. The question is not, whether such impatience is not open to the charge of wilfulness and self-conceit; but…whether there are not minds with ardent feelings, keen imaginations, and undisciplined tempers, who are under a strong irritation prompting them to run wild,—whether it is not our duty…to play with such, carefully letting out line enough lest they snap it,—and whether the Protestant Establishment is as indulgent and wise as might be desired in its treatment of such persons, inasmuch as it provides no occupation for them, does not understand how to turn them to account, lets them run to waste, tempts them to dissent, loses them, is weakened by the loss, and then denounces them.

But Antony benefited from a hierarchical Church which accepted his charism but gave it 'form…It was not vulgar, bustling, imbecile, unstable, undutiful; it was calm and composed…full of affectionate loyalty to the Church'. Newman makes the point explicitly that

---

[19] *HS* ii.96.

the charisms need the hierarchy: 'enthusiasm is sobered and refined by being submitted to the discipline of the Church, instead of being allowed to run wild externally to it'.[20] The danger, conversely, for the hierarchical Church is that without the charisms it risks losing vitality and becoming atrophied, with organization and routine replacing the Spirit.

In the *Essay on the Development of Doctrine*, Newman also writes of the monastic charism, where he is clear about the immense significance of this charism for the history of the Church: 'Little did the youth Antony foresee, when he set off to fight the evil one in the wilderness, what a sublime and various history he was opening, a history which had its first developments even in his own lifetime.' Antony had simply intended to be a hermit in the desert, 'but when others followed his example, he was obliged to give them guidance'. The next stage in the development was when these hermits came together to form a community. There followed further developments with St Pachomius and St Basil. And finally St Benedict consolidated these developments, as well as introducing the vital new element of education that was to be so crucial for the Church in the dark ages when the monasteries became the repositories of learning.[21]

As the future Pope Benedict xvi put it, 'apostolic movements appear in ever new forms in history—necessarily so, because they are the Holy Spirit's answer to the ever changing situations in which the Church lives'.[22] And this Newman saw quite clearly too. For he proceeded to point out that, while 'St. Benedict had come as if to preserve a principle of civilization, and a refuge for learning, at a time when the old framework of society was falling, and new political creations were taking their place... when the young intellect within them began to stir, and a change of another kind discovered itself, then appeared St. Francis and St. Dominic'. Finally, Newman concludes, 'in the last era of ecclesiastical revolution' the charism of St Ignatius made its appearance to meet new needs. 'The hermitage, the cloister... and the friar were suited to other states of society; with the Jesuits, as well as with the religious Communities, which are their juniors,' the 'chief objects of attention' were new kinds of apostolate, such as teaching and the missions.[23]

---

[20] *HS* ii.98–9, 103.   [21] *Dev.* 395–7.
[22] *Movements in the Church*, 46.   [23] *Dev.* 398–9.

There are half a dozen rhetorical passages in the *Essay on the Development of Christian Doctrine* where Newman sketches a picture of the early Church and asks the reader whether it is not also a likeness of the modern Roman Catholic Church. It is significant that in the first two of these passages it is the charismatic aspect which he singles out as the most characteristic feature in common. The first of these passages, in which Newman appeals to the imagination of the reader, begins with the provocative assertion: 'On the whole, all parties will agree that, of all existing systems, the present communion of Rome is the nearest approximation in fact to the Church of the Fathers, possible though some may think it, to be nearer still to that Church on paper.' He insists: 'Did St. Athanasius or St. Ambrose come suddenly to life, it cannot be doubted what communion he would take to be his own. All surely will agree that these Fathers…would find themselves more at home with such men as St. Bernard or St. Ignatius Loyola…or the holy sisterhood of mercy…'. And a couple of pages later he asks whether the faith of the Roman Catholic Church is not 'the nearest approach, to say the least, to the religious sentiment, and what is called *ethos*, of the early Church, nay, to that of the Apostles and Prophets; for all will agree so far as this, that Elijah, Jeremiah, the Baptist, and St. Paul are in their history and mode of life…in what is external and meets the eye…these saintly and heroic men, I say, are more like a Dominican preacher, or a Jesuit missionary, or a Carmelite friar, more like St. Toribio, or St. Vincent Ferrer, or St. Francis Xavier, or St. Alphonsus Liguori, than to any individuals, or to any classes of men, that can be found in other communions'.[24]

The success of the Oxford Movement raised one very serious problem. In 1839 Newman warned that there would be 'continual defections to Rome' unless the Church of England would allow the open expression of Catholic devotions and spirituality: 'give us monasteries', for example, he demanded. He discussed with Pusey his idea of a 'monastic house' out at Littlemore. Community life there began in 1842.[25] It was quasi-monastic, although Newman intended 'to master' the 'very instructive' *Spiritual Exercises* of St Ignatius Loyola; he admitted to finding the holiness particularly of the Jesuits disconcerting since his complaint that the Roman Church lacked sanctity was one of his last defences for his crumbling Anglicanism.[26] It was

---

[24] *Dev.* 97–8, 100.   [25] *LD* vii.133, 264.

[26] See Ian Ker, *John Henry Newman: A Biography* (Oxford: Clarendon Press, 1988), 271–2.

thus in the context of both the monastic and Ignatian charisms that three years later he finally decided to become a Roman Catholic. But the charism of St Francis had also played a role earlier in the process of conversion. In 1837 he had read with delight Manzoni's novel *I promesi sposi*. Two years later in September 1839, the year of his first serious doubts about Anglicanism, he admitted to one of his closest friends: 'That Capuchin in the "Promesi Sposi" has stuck in my heart like a dart. I have never got over him.' He was already considering religious life for himself: 'if things were to come to the worst, I should turn Brother of Charity in London—an object which, *quite* independently of any such perplexities, is growing on me, and, peradventure, will some day be accomplished...'[27] This remarkable letter was written shortly after the shock he had received from studying the Monophysite controversy during July and August, and a week before he again wrote to the same friend about the new blow he had received on reading an article on the Donatist controversy by Wiseman. In the *Apologia* Newman says nothing about the Capuchin friar in *Promesi sposi*, any more than he speaks of other experiences which contributed to his conversion; the book after all was intended to be about his intellectual not his imaginative history, being simply, in the words of the subtitle, 'a history of his religious opinions'.[28]

4

In 1847 Newman's dream of 1839 came (at least partly) true when he joined not a religious order but the Oratory of St Philip Neri. He was attracted by the charism of Philip, with his mixture of 'extreme hatred of humbug, playfulness, nay oddity, tender love for others, and severity'.[29] He was characterized by the same kind of Christian humanism as Newman's favourite Father, St Athanasius. Philip, too, who 'lived in an age...when literature and art were receiving their fullest development', was anxious 'not to destroy or supersede...but...to sanctify poetry, and history, and painting, and music'.[30] Charisms are for the good of the Church and Newman considered the charism of the

---

[27] *LD* vii.151.
[28] See Ian Ker, ed., *Apologia* (London: Penguin, 1994), xxi–xxiv.
[29] *LD* xii.25.   [30] *OS* 118–19.

Oratory to have been important in the Counter-Reformation for the much-needed reform of the secular clergy. But if Oratorians provided a model for the diocesan priesthood, nevertheless Newman saw them as quasi-religious, and, in spite of the very obvious differences, like the early monks in some respects, who also did not take vows. For Philip's charism was boldly to go back to primitive Christianity in its 'plainness and simplicity', not least in the informal 'exercises' which consisted of singing, prayer, readings, talks, and discussion, in which, extraordinarily for the time, laymen participated.[31] Newman liked to contrast Philip's charism with that of his contemporary Ignatius Loyola, whose followers were disciplined soldiers as compared with the individualistic, easy-going Oratorian.

Naturally, Newman had no illusion about which of the two charisms had been more important for the Church; in terms of influence and numbers there was no comparison between the Society of Jesus and the Oratory. In his 1850 sermon 'The Mission of St. Philip' he called Sts Benedict, Dominic, and Ignatius 'the three venerable Patriarchs, whose Orders divide between them the extent of Christian history'. Certainly, St Philip was a minor charismatic figure compared to these giants, but nevertheless Newman points out that he 'came under the teaching of all three successively'. Although he did not have the term 'charism' in his theological vocabulary and although he lived at a time when the importance of the hierarchical dimension of the Church was exaggerated, Newman never underestimated the significance of the charismatic dimension. For these 'masters in the spiritual Israel' had, 'in an especial way...had committed to them the office of a public ministry in the affairs of the Church one after another, and...are, in some sense, her "nursing fathers"'. From his youth in Florence at San Marco Philip imbibed the spirit of Dominic, whose vocation was 'to form the whole matter of human knowledge into one harmonious system, to secure the alliance between religion and philosophy, and to train men to the use of the gifts of nature in the sunlight of divine grace and revealed truth'. This Christian humanism was essential in Philip's age, the age of the Renaissance, when 'a violent effort was in progress...to break up this sublime unity, and to set human genius, the philosopher and the poet, the artist and the musician, in opposition to religion'. Leaving

---

31 *NO* 186, 188, 203.

Florence, Philip came to live near Monte Cassino, where in turn he imbibed the simpler Benedictine spirit: 'and, as from St. Dominic he gained the end he was to pursue, so from St. Benedict he learned how to pursue it'. The Oratory resembled those early independent monastic communities without formal vows and not organized in an order, which 'were simple in their forms of worship, and...freely admitted laymen into their fellowship'. Finally, Philip met St Ignatius in Rome, with whom 'in the care of souls he was one', as 'in theological traditions [he] was one with St. Dominic'. Newman sums up the influence on Philip of these three great charisms: 'As then he learned from Benedict *what to be*, and from Dominic *what to do*, so let me consider that from Ignatius he learned *how he was to do it*.' To these he contributed his own special charism: '[he] had the breadth of view of St. Dominic, the poetry of St. Benedict, the wisdom of St. Ignatius, and all recommended by an unassuming grace and a winning tenderness which were his own'.[32]

In 1855 Newman gave a lecture to the Birmingham Catholic Association entitled 'The Three Patriarchs of Christian History, St Benedict, St Dominic, and St Ignatius', of which some notes survive.[33] He had had it in mind to write a book, as he put it in 1870, on the 'historical contrast of Benedictines, Dominicans, and Jesuits, which I suppose I shall never finish'. In the end, he only managed to write the part on the Benedictines, which was first published in the *Atlantis*, the academic journal he founded at the Catholic University of Ireland, and then republished in the second volume of *Historical Sketches*.[34] It was a source of regret to him, as he explained later, but, when the Abbot of Solesmes criticized what he had written on the Benedictines,

> I felt that if I continued my journey into Dominican, Franciscan, and Jesuit territory, I could not be true unless I mastered a great mass of reading...One question was already asked me, viz. why I confined my review of teaching Orders to Benedictine, Dominican, and Jesuits, omitting Franciscans. I had my reasons. I thought them men of genius rather than systematic teaching or normal authority, viewed as a body; but I ought to have read a great deal to maintain this view; and in consequence I never have been confident in the correctness of my view myself.[35]

---

[32] *OS* 220–1, 224–5, 228, 240.   [33] See *LD* xvi.378.
[34] *LD* xxv.228.   [35] *LD* xxviii.130

One can only regret that Newman was never able to complete this book on these three great charismatic movements in the history of the Church; and perhaps if he could have read more he might have included the Franciscans—but as we have seen the Franciscan charism had played a small role in the process of his conversion.

'The Mission of the Benedictine Order' was published in the *Atlantis* in 1858 and 'The Benedictine Centuries' in 1859; they were republished in *Historical Sketches* in 1873 under the titles of 'The Mission of St. Benedict' and 'The Benedictine Schools'. Unlike the Church of the Fathers this was not a period of history he knew well. His concern was chiefly educational, occupied as he was with the Catholic University; but, even apart from that, as he once wrote, 'from first to last, education...has been my line'.[36] The history of Christian education could be divided into three periods, ancient, medieval, and modern, dominated by the names of Benedict, Dominic, and Ignatius; clearly Francis could not compete with them in this sphere. The monastic charism was 'a reaction from...secular life', a 'flight from the world', it offered 'retirement and repose...peace'. It was a 'poetical' charism, unlike the Dominican which was 'scientific' and the Ignatian which was 'practical'. Monasticism evoked the 'primitive age of the world' and 'was a sort of recognized emigration from the old world' ever since St Antony had found 'gold...and on the news of it thousands took their departure year after year for the diggings in the desert'. It was more devotional than intellectual. But the charism was poetical not because the monks were 'dreamy sentimentalists, to fall in love with melancholy winds and purling rills, and waterfalls and nodding groves; but their poetry was the poetry of hard work', since Benedict's 'object...was...penance'. Still, monasticism was 'romantic' in its 'adventures' and history. The paradox was that the very monasticism which had been a retreat from a dying world became 'in no small measure [the] very life' of the 'new order'.[37] So far as Newman was concerned, it was not the hierarchy but the charism of one man, who was not even a priest, that had saved Christian civilization.

---

[36] *AW* 259.   [37] *HS* ii.366, 373, 375, 384–5, 388, 398, 400, 436, 443.

5

If Newman can be called the 'Father of the Second Vatican Council' and if the new ecclesial communities and movements are, so to speak, the charismatic accompaniment of that Council, rather as the Jesuits embodied the spirit of the Council of Trent, then one would not be surprised to find that Newman anticipated this charismatic phenomenon of the twentieth century.

Tractarianism was itself a self-proclaimed 'movement' and, like the ecclesial movements, was neither clerical nor lay, but a movement of the baptized. The original initiative was entirely clerical, the idea being to form a society of clergy centred on Oxford, but with branches all over the country. However, Newman wanted a movement not a clerical association, and he was strongly opposed especially to any kind of clerical committee or board supervising the *Tracts for the Times*, which were his idea. Instead, he wanted the *Tracts* to be circulated by personal contact and to be personally written by individuals.[38] As he was to put it in the *Apologia*, 'Living Movements do not come of committees.'[39] As in the new ecclesial movements, the emphasis was to be upon the personal and charismatic rather than the institutional and structural.

Nor were theological tracts the only form of literature that the Tractarians employed. Newman characteristically saw that the movement must have an imaginative as well as an intellectual appeal. Accordingly, he and his collaborators soon began publishing 'Records of the Church', or what he called 'little stories of the Apostles, fathers etc., to familiarize the imagination of the reader to an *Apostolical state* of the Church.'[40] Clearly this kind of propaganda was intended at least as much for the laity as for the clergy. The same was true of the *Lyra Apostolica*, the verse section in the *British Magazine* which he and Hurrell Froude had conceived of a year before the Oxford Movement proper began, hoping to advance their ideas through what Newman called the 'rhetoric' and 'persuasion' of poetry.[41] When the verses were published in book form in 1836, Newman was amazed by their remarkable success in advancing 'Apostolical views', as he told his friend Maria Giberne, who was herself involved in the movement. He was keen that she should try her hand at writing 'some Apostolical

---

[38]   See Ker, *John Henry Newman*, 81, 84–5.   [39]   *Apo.* 46.
[40]   *LD* iv.109.   [41]   *LD* iii.121.

stories' for children and hoped that she could collaborate with his sister Jemima and sister-in-law Anne Mozley. What he thought was really needed was 'a library on all subjects for the middle classes and the Clergy'.[42] In other words, he wanted the movement to be propagated by every possible kind of writing, for the laity as well as the clergy, and for women and children as well as men. Since fiction was becoming a particularly effective medium of communication and since practitioners of the art were often women (including Newman's own sister Harriett, herself a successful author of children's books), lay women played a significant role in the movement. If the leading Tractarian poet was a clergyman, John Keble, the leading Tractarian novelist was to be a lay woman, Charlotte M. Yonge.

Newman was struck by the fact that prominent precursors of the movement like Alexander Knox, the Irish theologian, and the Romantic philosopher and poet Samuel Taylor Coleridge were both 'laymen and that is very remarkable', as was Dr Johnson, 'another striking instance'.[43] Many of the leading members of the Oxford Movement were laymen, often prominent in public life. It was the absence of this kind of easy collaboration between clergy and laity that impressed Newman so unfavourably when he became a Catholic.

On the restoration of the Roman Catholic hierarchy to England in 1850, a storm of anti-Catholicism erupted. Newman's response to the orchestrated campaign against Catholics is interesting. He thought that it could be profitably exploited by making it an excuse for 'getting up a great organization, going round the towns giving lectures, or making speeches... starting a paper, a review etc.'. He recommended gathering laymen to speak at public meetings in the big towns. Young Catholics particularly, he felt, should band together as the Tractarians had. In short, he saw the possibility of another movement, the occasion being again the persecution of the Church, albeit a different one. This time the condemnations of the *Tracts* and the suspensions of preachers by the authorities might be matched by the threatened fining, imprisonment, and even transportation of recalcitrant Catholic bishops. But, as in the past, Newman sadly realized that the bishops would not rise to the occasion. However, now his main complaint was that the Catholic hierarchy had not bothered nor did they intend to consult the laity on the best course of action to take.

---

[42] *LD* v.385, 387; vi.32.   [43] *LD* v.27.

Newman, in fact, had a clear understanding of the original charism of the Oratory of St Philip Neri, the character of which is unmistakably similar to the new ecclesial communities. To counter the anti-Catholic agitation, he embarked on a series of public lectures in June 1851. They were published in book form as *Lectures on the Present Position of Catholics in England: Addressed to the Brothers of the Oratory*. These brothers constituted the so-called 'Little' or 'Secular' Oratory, which was the confraternity of laymen traditionally attached to an Oratory. (Newman got permission from Rome for a separate one for women.[44]) Of all the Oratorian activities and works, Newman, remarkably, considered this as 'more important than anything else'.[45] What Newman had in mind was that the Oratory, after all, had started in Rome as a lay community. But then, in Newman's words,

> a smaller society was formed in addition to this and by a closer tie. Its members actually lived together, they were priests, or those who were training for the priesthood, and they served the Church. It was this Community which was erected into a Congregation, under the title of the Congregation of the Oratory.
>
> The Oratory itself, however, remained as before, with its own rules and members, taking the place of a sort of confraternity dependent on the Congregation, and governed by it, and for distinction [sic] sake being called the Oratorium parvum or the Oratorium externum. It still had possession of the building called the Oratorium, while the place of the Congregation rather was the Church...[46]

This development, in fact, is similar to the way in which out of the new ecclesial communities (and movements) there regularly emerges a smaller more committed group, such as priests or consecrated men and women (or the equivalent), but still closely linked with the larger group which supports it but which in turn is sustained by this inner core of members. By Newman's day, the 'little Oratory' had become a shadow of its former self. In reality, the Oratory had undergone the same kind of clericalization as the Benedictines and Franciscans who were invariably ordained, if at all possible, to the priesthood, even though neither Benedict nor Francis had been priests. Similarly, the original charism of the Oratory had become obscured as the Oratory simply became a congregation of priests, although like other orders and congregations it had lay brothers, who did the menial tasks in the

⁴⁴ See *LD* xvii.137–8.   ⁴⁵ *LD* xiv.274.   ⁴⁶ *NO* 164.

community and were seen as second-class members. But Newman knew this was unfaithful to Philip's charism. As he wrote sharply in a letter of rebuke to a priest in the Birmingham Oratory, 'The Brothers are our equals... The Father is above the Brother sacerdotally—but in the Oratory they are equal.'[47]

The ecclesiology of organic communion that we find in *On Consulting the Faithful in Matters of Doctrine* is, as we have seen, that of *Lumen Gentium*, an ecclesiology which finds concrete realization in the new ecclesial communities and movements.[48] As an Anglican, as we have seen in Chapter 2 and to repeat what was said there,[49] Newman had learned from the Greek Fathers that the Church is primarily the communion of those who have received the Holy Spirit in baptism. While the Church 'is a visible body', and therefore has the character of an institution, it is nevertheless 'invested with, or... existing in invisible privileges', for 'the Church would cease to be the Church, did the Holy Spirit leave it', since 'its outward rites and forms are nourished and animated by the living power which dwells within it'. Thus the Church is the Holy Spirit's 'especial dwelling-place'. For while Christ came 'to die for us; the Spirit came to make us one in Him who had died and was alive, that is, to form the Church'. The Church, then, is 'the one mystical body of Christ... quickened by the Spirit'—and is 'one' by virtue of the Holy Spirit 'giving it life'.[50]

Similarly, when, as a Catholic towards the end of his life, Newman wrote a very lengthy new preface to his Anglican *Lectures on the Prophetical Office of the Church*, in which he answered the charge in the lectures that there is a discordance between the Roman Catholic Church's 'formal teaching and its popular and political manifestations', it is striking how he takes as his starting point not the institutional but the sacramental understanding of the Church as Christ's 'mystical Body and Bride... and the shrine and organ of the Paraclete'.[51] Given the nineteenth-century Tridentine idea of the Church as first foremost the hierarchical Church militant, it might be supposed that Newman would have explained this kind of contradiction or corruption in terms of such a Church. Surely the most obvious explanation would have been to point out that the Catholic belief that the pope and bishops were the successors of Peter and the other Apostles meant that

---

[47] *LD* xvi.267.   [48] See Chapter 3, section 3, p. 83.
[49] See Chapter 2, section 3, p. 61.
[50] *PS* iii.224; v.41; iii.270; iv.170, 174, 171.   [51] *VM* i.xxxvii, xxxix.

inevitably such hierarchical power was open to corruption in a way that the Protestant ministry with its much more modest claims was not. A Catholic clergy was naturally tempted to abuse its much greater authority by tolerating, even encouraging, superstition as a means of controlling the faithful, while episcopal and papal authority could easily be misused in order to extend the Church's power. But instead of speaking about the Church in terms of clergy and laity, the Preface begins by describing the Church as the Body of Christ, which therefore shares in the three 'offices' of Christ as prophet, priest, and king. The discrepancies between the theory and the practice of Catholicism are the result of the difficulties of exercising this 'triple office' simultaneously. The prophetical office is seen as belonging pre-eminently to theologians, but nothing is said about whether they are clerical or lay. Nor even is the priestly office 'particularly assigned to the ordained, as one might have expected'. Instead, 'initially' Newman 'attributes this office to the "pastor and flock", but in the main body of the Preface he focuses almost entirely on popular religion and on the beliefs of the simple faithful'.[52]

Similarly, again, *Lumen Gentium*, rejecting the Tridentine model of the Church as first and foremost hierarchical, begins with a chapter on 'The Mystery of the Church', in which the Church is conceived of being 'in the nature of sacrament' (art. 1). As in Newman, the Church is the Church because of the Holy Spirit: 'The Spirit dwells in the Church and in the hearts of the faithful as in a temple' (art. 4). The second chapter called 'The People of God' is no more about the laity specifically than the first chapter was concerned with the hierarchy, for this people consists of those who have received the Holy Spirit in baptism, a 'messianic people' in whom the Spirit 'dwells as in a temple' (art. 9). This 'priestly community is brought into operation through the sacraments', and, as we saw in Chapter 3, it is only after the sacraments of initiation followed by the sacraments of penance and anointing which all the baptized normally receive have been mentioned, that the constitution refers to two sacraments that not all the faithful receive, holy orders and marriage (art. 11). It is not, then, only that the Church is not conceived of primarily in hierarchical terms but the whole concept of clergy and laity is avoided in these

---

[52] Avery Dulles, SJ, 'The Threefold Office in Newman's Ecclesiology', in Ian Ker and Alan G. Hill, eds, *Newman after a Hundred Years* (Oxford: Clarendon Press, 1990), 380.

first two thoroughly scriptural and patristic chapters that describe the fundamental nature of the Church, which does not primarily consist of clergy and laity (plus religious) but of all the baptized. Now if we turn to the ecclesial communities and movements, we find exactly the same avoidance of the usual clerical way of looking at the Church. This is why, as we have seen,[53] to call them lay movements and communities is radically to misunderstand them. On the contrary, they are truly 'ecclesial'. Faithful to the organic conception of the Church as described in *Lumen Gentium* and as understood by Newman, these movements of the Spirit are, in the words of Piero Coda, a theologian belonging to the Focolare movement, 'constitutionally open (by virtue of their original charism) to all the vocations and to all the states of life present in the People of God'. Coda calls the classification of them as 'lay' mere 'inertia of reflection'.[54] In fact, the description reflects that very ecclesiology which perceives the Church in clerical-lay terms that the first two chapters of *Lumen Gentium* carefully avoided. The ecclesial movements and communities are 'ecclesial' precisely because they share the same ecclesiology of organic wholeness. They consist of bishops, priests, religious, and lay people, as well as those who are so committed to the charism of the particular movement or community as to be quasi-religious, albeit without formal vows.[55]

The future Pope Benedict XVI was certain that this new phenomenon in the life of the Church represents the fifth great charismatic movement of the Spirit in the history of the Church, in succession to the monasticism of the third century, the mendicant friars of the thirteenth, the Jesuits and other active orders in the sixteenth, and the missionary congregations of the nineteenth.[56] The fact that the ecclesial movements and communities embody the ecclesiology of the first two chapters of *Lumen Gentium* is not surprising. For charisms are given to the Church by the Holy Spirit in response to the particular historical situations in which the Church finds herself.[57]

---

[53] See Chapter 3, section 3, p. 82–3. [54] *Movements in the Church*, 95.
[55] For a fuller discussion, see Ian Ker, *The New Movements: A Theological Introduction* (London: Catholic Truth Society, 2001), reprinted in a slightly abridged version under the title 'New Movements and Communities in the Life of the Church' in *Louvain Studies* 27 (2002), 69–95.
[56] Joseph Cardinal Ratzinger, 'The Ecclesial Movements: A Theological Reflection on their Place in the Church', in *Movements in the Church*, 23–51.
[57] See section 3, p. 94.

The charism of Ignatius appeared providentially at the time of the Council of Trent. The letter of Councils needs the Spirit. The new ecclesial movements and communities have not arisen as a humanly planned response to the Second Vatican Council's renewed understanding of the nature of the Church, but they surely do represent the response of the Holy Spirit. And, as we have seen, Newman not only had the same understanding of the Church, but he himself inspired and led what was called a movement and then joined himself to the charism of the Oratory of St Philip, which in its original form seems so extraordinarily contemporary today. But perhaps that is not so surprising when one considers how Philip also, like Newman and the Council, wanted to return to a more primitive and scriptural Catholicism, such as the new movements and communities themselves manifest. Free of the clericalism that Newman so deplored in the nineteenth-century Church, they are also free of its opposite, what I call 'laicism', that post-conciliar phenomenon that Newman would no less have deplored. The truth is that both clericalism and 'laicism' feel threatened by charisms, and that alone is an important reason for the Church never to lose sight of its charismatic dimension.

5

Some Unintended Consequences
of Vatican II

1

Vatican II's Constitution on Divine Revelation is, alongside the Constitution on the Church, the other most important dogmatic document produced by the Council. *Dei Verbum* declares at the outset that through revelation 'the deepest truth about God and the salvation of man is made clear to us in Christ, who is the Mediator and at the same time the fullness of all revelation' (art. 2). It then proceeds to state, quoting Vatican I, that faith 'must be given to God who reveals, an obedience by which man entrusts his whole self freely to God, offering "the full submission of intellect and will to God who reveals," and freely assenting to the truth revealed by Him' (art. 5). The Council wanted to make it clear that the Christian revelation is not so much a series of dogmatic propositions as the revealing of God in Christ to whom, rather than to a set of propositions, we are required to give not merely an intellectual assent but the commitment of our whole self. In other words, both revelation and faith are primarily of a personalistic rather than propositional nature. If the understanding of revelation and faith was overly propositional before the Council, the pendulum now swung to the opposite extreme, as Newman could have predicted. It was in this anti-propositional theological climate that a book could actually appear entitled *Has Dogma a Future?* by a well-known theologian.[1] This climate explains the widespread hostility to Pope John Paul II's decision in 1985 that a *Catechism of the*

---

[1] Gerald O'Collins, SJ, *Has Dogma a Future?* (London: Darton, Longman & Todd, 1975).

Catholic Church should be published, as it duly was nine years later.
By that time this anti-propositional theology had well and truly per-
colated down to the level of the parish and school, with very serious
consequences for catechesis and preaching.

Newman himself was emphatic both as an Anglican and as a
Catholic that the Christian revelation is fundamentally personalistic
rather than propositional. For God reveals himself rather than truths
about himself in the person of the incarnate Jesus Christ. Newman
declared as a Catholic: 'What Catholics, what Church doctors, as well
as Apostles, have ever lived on, is not any number of theological can-
ons or decrees, but...the Christ Himself, as He is represented in concrete existence in the Gospels.'[2] This was consonant with his earlier
approach as an Anglican:

> As God is one, so the impression which He gives us of Himself is one;
> it is not a thing of parts; it is not a system...It is the vision of an object.
> When we pray, we pray, not to an assemblage of notions, or to a creed,
> but to One Individual Being; and when we speak of Him we speak of a
> Person...This being the case, all our attempts to delineate our impres-
> sion of Him go to bring out one idea, not two or three or four; not a
> philosophy, but an individual idea in its separate aspects.

Our experience of God revealed in Christ is not, of course, an immediate one as it was for the Apostles, but is mediated to us through their
unique experience of the reality: 'The ideas which we are granted of
Divine Objects under the Gospel, from the nature of the case and
because they are ideas, answer to the Originals so far as this, that they
are whole, indivisible, substantial, and may be called real, as being
images of what is real.'[3]

But if Newman's theology of revelation was fundamentally personalistic rather than propositional, that did not mean that he was in any
way anti-propositional and therefore anti-dogmatic. As he wrote in
the *Apologia*, from the time of his conversion in 1816 he could not
conceive of a religion that was not dogmatic.[4] Revelation may be primarily of a person, but a person speaks, and 'Why should God speak,
unless He meant to say something? Why should He say it, unless He
meant us to hear?' If there has been a revelation, than 'there must be
some essential doctrine proposed by it to our faith'. In other words,
'Religion cannot but be dogmatic; it ever has been.'[5] Revelation may

² DA 388.   ³ US 330.   ⁴ Apo. 54.   ⁵ DA 130–1, 134.

be primarily a 'vision', but is also a 'message'.[6] For the gospel 'is no mere philosophy thrown upon the world at large, no mere quality of mind and thought, no mere beautiful and deep sentiment or subjective opinion, but a substantive message from above'.[7]

Newman had never doubted the necessity of dogmatic propositions, but to begin with he had seen them as little more than an unfortunate necessity. In the *Arians*, he had held that 'freedom from symbols [i.e. creeds] and articles is abstractedly the highest state of Christian communion, and the peculiar privilege of the primitive Church', for 'technicality and formalism are, in their degree, inevitable results of public confessions of faith', and 'when confessions do not exist, the mysteries of divine truth, instead of being exposed to the gaze of the profane and uninstructed, are kept hidden in the bosom of the Church, far more faithfully than is otherwise possible'. However, Newman recognized that dogmatic definitions are both inevitable and necessary, although 'the rulers of the [early] Church were dilatory in applying a remedy, which nevertheless the circumstances of the time imperatively required. They were loath to confess, that the Church had grown too old to enjoy the free, unsuspicious teaching with which her childhood was blest'.[8]

Newman's lack of enthusiasm for dogmatic propositions at this stage partly resulted from his awareness of the inability of human language to speak adequately of revelation. His study of the Alexandrian Fathers had introduced him to the theology of Clement and Origen, which was 'based on the mystical or sacramental principle, and spoke of the various Economies or Dispensations of the Eternal'. Consequently, the Church's 'mysteries are but the expressions in human language of truths to which the human mind is unequal'.[9] The principle of economy meant that the doctrine of the Trinity, for example, in words already quoted,[10] is to be seen only as 'the shadow, projected for the contemplation of the intellect, of the Object of scripturally-informed piety: a representation, economical; necessarily imperfect, as being exhibited in a foreign medium, and therefore involving apparent inconsistencies or mysteries'. 'Systematic' dogma could be 'kept in the background in the infancy of Christianity, when faith and obedience were vigorous', only to be 'brought forward at a time when, reason being disproportionately developed, and aiming at

---

[6] DA 296.   [7] *Diff.* ii.236.   [8] *Ari.* 36–7.   [9] *Apo.* 36–7.
[10] See Chapter 2, section 2, p. 46.

sovereignty in the province of religion, its presence became necessary to expel an usurping idol from the house of God'. But from the point of view of the individual believer, to make explicit what was implicit was not necessarily desirable: 'So reluctant is a well-constituted mind to reflect on its own motive principles, that the correct intellectual image, from its hardness of outline, may startle and offend those who have all along been acting upon it.' But having indicated how undesirable dogmatic formulations are, Newman proceeds immediately to show how necessary they are: for the fact that 'we cannot restrain the rovings of the intellect, or silence its clamorous demand for a formal statement concerning the Object of our worship' means paradoxically that the insistence that 'intellectual representation should ever be subordinate to the cultivation of the religious affections' actually demands the 'intellectual expression of theological truth', not only because it 'excludes heresy', but because it 'directly assists the acts of religious worship and obedience'.[11] This was the beginning of a more positive attitude to doctrinal formulations.

Two years after the publication of the *Arians*, in *Tract 73, On the Introduction of Rationalistic Principles into Religion*, Newman explained, as we have seen,[12] that human language was inherently incapable of expressing adequately the truths of divine revelation, since these truths were mysteries which could not be fully comprehended by the human mind: 'No revelation can be complete and systematic, from the weakness of the human intellect; *so far as* it is not such, it is mysterious...'. Nor could they be adequately expressed in human language, which was 'the only possible medium', but only 'according to the capacity of language' and therefore had, as it were, to lie '*hid* in language'. Revelation, therefore, was 'religious doctrine viewed on its illuminated side', while as a mystery it was 'the selfsame doctrine viewed on the side unilluminated':

> Thus Religious Truth is neither light nor darkness, but both together; it is like the dim view of a country seen in the twilight, with forms half extracted from the darkness, with broken lines, and isolated masses. Revelation...is not a revealed *system*, but consists of a number of detached and incomplete truths belonging to a vast system unrevealed, of doctrines and injunctions mysteriously connected together.[13]

---

[11] *Ari.* 145–6. [12] See Chapter 1, section I.4, p. 12.
[13] *Ess.* i.41–2.

Three years later, in *Lectures on the Doctrine of Justification*, doctrinal propositions are still viewed as more negative than positive. Necessary and useful as 'landmarks' and summaries of belief, they are 'intended to forbid speculations, which are sure to spring up in the human mind, and to anticipate its attempts at systematic views by showing the ultimate abyss at which all rightly conducted inquiries arrive, not to tell us anything definite and real, which we did not know before, or which is beyond the faith of the most unlearned.'[14]

By the time, however, that Newman came in 1843 to write the last of the *Oxford University Sermons* on 'The Theory of Developments in Religious Doctrine', the formulation of dogmatic propositions is viewed in a much more positive light, because now doctrinal development is seen as a sign of life in the Church. It is true that doctrinal statements are said to be 'necessary only because the human mind cannot reflect... except piecemeal' upon 'the one idea which they are designed to express', so that they are only expressions of 'aspects' of the 'idea' and 'can never really be confused with the idea itself, which all such propositions taken together can but reach, and cannot exceed', and indeed to which they are 'never equivalent'—for 'dogmas are, after all, but symbols of a Divine fact, which, far from being compassed by those very propositions, would not be exhausted, nor fathomed, by a thousand'. On the other hand, dogmatic definitions are seen as essential for *realizing* the Christian revelation. There is no contradiction between a personal faith in Christ and a dogmatic creed because the latter only seeks to give expression and substance to the former:

> That idea is not enlarged, if propositions are added... with a view of conveying that one integral view, not of amplifying it. That view does not depend on such propositions: it does not consist in them; they are but specimens and indications of it. And they may be multiplied without limit. They are necessary, but not needful to it, being but portions or aspects of that previous impression which has at length come under the cognizance of Reason and the terminology of science... One thing alone has to be impressed on us by Scripture, the Catholic idea, and in it they are all included. To object, then, to the number of propositions, upon which an anathema is placed, is altogether to mistake their use; for their multiplication is not intended to enforce many things, but to express one.[15]

---

[14] *Jfc.* 316.   [15] *US* 331–2, 336.

The 'Catholic idea' may seem impersonal, but the 'idea' of course is of the person of Christ. Nearly thirty years later, in *An Essay in Aid of a Grammar of Assent* (1870), Newman provided a classic statement of the relationship between personal faith in a person and doctrinal propositions. He criticized 'the common mistake of supposing that there is a contrariety and antagonism between a dogmatic creed and vital religion' in a passage which should have been compulsory reading for catechists and religious educators after Vatican II:

> People urge that salvation consists, not in believing the propositions that there is a God, that there is a Saviour, that our Lord is God, that there is a Trinity, but in believing in God, in a Saviour, in a Sanctifier; and they object that such propositions are but a formal and human medium destroying all true reception of the Gospel, and making religion a matter of words or of logic, instead of its having its seat in the heart. They are right so far as this, that men can and sometimes do rest in the propositions themselves as expressing intellectual notions; they are wrong, when they maintain that men need to do so or always do so. The propositions may and must be used, and can easily be used, as the expression of facts, not notions, and they are necessary to the mind in the same way that language is ever necessary for denoting facts, both for ourselves as individuals, and for our intercourse with others. Again, they are useful in their dogmatic aspect as ascertaining and making clear for us the truths on which the religious imagination has to rest. Knowledge must ever precede the exercise of the affections. We feel gratitude and love, we feel indignation and dislike, when we have the informations actually put before us which are to kindle those several emotions. We love our parents, as our parents, when we know them to be our parents; we must know concerning God, before we can feel love, fear, hope, or trust towards Him. Devotion must have its objects; those objects, as being supernatural, when not represented to our senses by material symbols, must be set before the mind in propositions. The formula, which embodies a dogma for the theologian, readily suggests an object for the worshipper.[16]

The dogmatic formulations that Newman had once seen as necessary but undesirable are now seen as indispensable for personal faith. Newman now realizes that dogma not only protects religion from error, but is in fact integral to faith, which cannot exist without knowledge of its object of worship. Of course, he knew when he

---

[16] *GA* 82–3.

wrote the *Arians* that the believer cannot worship Christ without *some* knowledge of who Christ is, but he seemed to think that it was a pity that the faith could not rest on the simplest kind of *kerugma*. But nearly forty years later he is very clear that, far from there being any kind of opposition between a personalistic and a prepositional faith, the two are in fact indivisible.

However, Newman also understood that it is not possible to list all the doctrines which a Catholic is required to believe. The Church, he pointed out, 'would be misrepresenting the real character of the dispensation' and 'abdicating her function' by transferring the faith of Catholics 'from resting on herself as the organ of revelation... simply to a code of certain definite articles or a written creed'. For 'the object of faith is *not* simply certain articles... contained in the dumb documents, but the whole word of God, explicit and implicit, as dispensed by His living Church'.[17] Newman likens the Church to 'a standing Apostolic committee—to answer questions which the Apostles are not here to answer, concerning what they received and preached'.[18] A Catholic's faith, then, is not ultimately in formulations and propositions but in the living Church.

2

The Pastoral Constitution on the Church in the Modern World, *Gaudium et Spes*, is by far the longest of the documents of the Second Vatican Council. It is also the one that would surely have caused Newman the greatest misgivings, not so much for what it says—or rather fails to say, for he would certainly have been disturbed by its optimistic tone and the lack of emphasis on the sin of 'this world' (Jn 12:31) and 'the evil one' (1 Jn 2:13)—as for the likely if unintended effect of the Council producing such a long and ambitious document on 'the presence and activity of the Church in the world of today' (art. 2). On the one hand, Newman would have been delighted by the Christian humanism of the striking affirmation that 'only in the mystery of the Incarnate Word does the mystery of man take on light' (art.

---

[17] *LD* xxiii.99–100, 105.   [18] *LD* xxv.418.

22). On the other hand, he would have been very alive to the danger of a phrase like 'the autonomy of earthly affairs' (art. 36) being taken out of context to encourage a quasi-secular humanism within the Church. *Gaudium et Spes* called for the establishment of an 'agency of the universal Church...for the world-wide promotion of justice for the poor' (art. 90), which led to the creation of what is now called the Pontifical Council for Justice and Peace, a department of the Roman Curia. Individual dioceses also established equivalent offices and justice and peace groups became common in parishes. Now obviously Newman would have had no difficulty with the laudable aim of promoting justice and peace in the world. But what he would have feared was the danger of justice and peace becoming a kind of rival gospel to or substitute for the gospel of the crucified and risen Christ. And he would not have been in the least surprised that a kind of religion of justice and peace came in the years after the Council to be more or less practically identified with the gospel in not a few quarters of the Church. After all, he had written about an analogous danger in his own day.

In the eighth Discourse of *The Idea of a University*, 'Knowledge viewed in relation to Religion', Newman warned that the 'intellectual culture' which he had been advocating at such length and so eloquently as the end of a university education could easily become the rival of religion. The 'educated mind' had, he acknowledged, a kind of 'religion of its own, independent of Catholicism, partly co-operating with it, partly thwarting it'. While reason 'rightly exercised' led 'the mind to the Catholic Faith', it was 'far from taking so straight and satisfactory a direction' in practice. Reason, Newman warned, 'makes a religion for itself' even when it accepted Catholicism. For this 'Religion of Reason' or 'Religion of Civilization' was 'simply distinct' from Catholicism. It could be an ally of Catholicism in 'drawing the mind off from things which will harm it to subjects which are worthy a rational being', having 'a natural tendency to refine the mind, and to give it...a disgust and abhorrence' for 'excesses and enormities of evil'. There were many virtues that 'intellectual culture' could produce 'and all upon the type of Christianity'. But, Newman insisted, there was a 'radical difference' from 'genuine religion'. In the latter conscience excites fear which 'implies the transgression of a law, and a law implies a lawgiver and judge'; whereas in the 'Religion of Reason' conscience excites merely shame, 'when the mind is simply angry with itself and nothing more...and a false philosophy has misinterpreted emotions which ought to lead to God', for 'the tendency of intellectual culture is to swallow up the fear in the self-reproach, and self-reproach is directed and limited to our mere sense of what is fitting and becoming', with the result that conscience becomes merely 'a moral sense or taste'.[19]

This 'Religion of Philosophy' contained not a single doctrine, Newman admitted, 'which is not in a certain sense true'—and yet 'almost every statement is perverted and made false, because it is not the whole truth'.[20] Analogously, no one could deny that the pursuit of justice and peace is highly commendable or that it is a highly Christian preoccupation. But the fact remains that it is not the whole of Christianity—which is centred anyway not on such moral abstractions but on the person of the crucified and risen Christ. Besides, it is not necessary to be a Christian to be in favour of justice and peace. Newman's acute sense of the unintended consequences of Councils[21] would surely have alerted him to the threat posed by such a long and compelling document as *Gaudium et Spes* of a veritable religion of justice and peace infiltrating and even taking over parts of the Church, a very attractive and plausible religion because so eminently Christian in its goals—but nevertheless not the religion of St Paul: 'And so, while the Jews demand miracles and the Greeks look for wisdom, here are we preaching a crucified Christ; to the Jews an obstacle that they cannot get over, to the pagans madness' (1 Cor. 1:23). But however absurd and mad such a manifesto seemed to the educated and religious world of his time, we can be sure that if St Paul had instead concentrated on the moral implications of Christian belief—such as justice and peace—or in other words had put the cart before the horse, Christians would have remained a tiny sect that the Roman Empire could comfortably have ignored. For in that case there would have been no 'news', the 'good news' that a man had risen from the dead, to disturb the *status quo*.

---

[19] *Idea* 161, 164–6.   [20] *Idea* 172.
[21] See Chapter 3, section 1, p. 80.

3

The concept of conscience that Newman distinguishes from the merely moral sense is somewhat briefly addressed in *Gaudium et Spes*: 'In the depths of his conscience, man detects a law which he does not impose upon himself, but which holds him to obedience...Conscience is the most secret core and sanctuary of a man. There he is alone with God, whose voice echoes in his depths.' Even when conscience 'errs from invincible ignorance', the Council insists that it does so 'without losing its dignity' (art. 16). This insistence on the primacy of conscience, although a thoroughly traditional Catholic teaching, nevertheless aroused a great deal of attention at the time and was widely misinterpreted to mean that Catholics were free to 'dissent conscientiously', as it was said, from Church teachings. Needless to say, there is nothing in the text of *Gaudium et Spes* to justify such an interpretation. However, the fact is that the Constitution, which is concerned here with conscience in general and not specifically the conscience of Catholics, does not say at this point what *Dignitatis Humanae* makes clear:

> In the formation of their consciences, the Christian faithful ought carefully to attend to the sacred and certain doctrine of the Church. The Church is, by the will of Christ, the teacher of the truth. It is her duty to give utterance to, and authoritatively to teach, that Truth which is Christ Himself, and also to declare and confirm by her authority those principles of the moral order which have their origin in human nature itself. (art. 14)

But, again, this was one of those unintentional consequences of Councils that Newman had noted, where what mattered was not what was said but what was not said. And in this instance Newman himself would have found himself regularly invoked in support of the idea that Vatican II upheld the right of Catholics to follow their consciences in rejecting teachings of the magisterium, a widespread idea to which we must now turn.

There are two very famous and important treatments of conscience in Newman's writings. The first is in his *An Essay in Aid of a Grammar of Assent* (1870), where Newman presents the argument from conscience for the existence of God. There he points out that conscience has two aspects: 'it is a moral sense, and a sense of duty; a judgment of the reason and a magisterial dictate', it 'has both a critical and judicious office'. It is in the latter aspect of a 'sanction' rather than a 'rule' of right conduct that conscience is primary, for it is as 'a voice, or the echo of a voice, imperative and constraining', that conscience is unique in our experience.[22]

Five years later Newman published his *Letter to the Duke of Norfolk* (1875), where he now deals with the relation of conscience to authority, in particular the relation of a Catholic conscience to the magisterium of the Church. Again, Newman is concerned with conscience as primarily a 'sense of duty', a 'magisterial dictate' rather than as a 'moral sense', a 'judgment of reason'.

To understand correctly the argument of the *Letter to the Duke of Norfolk* it is important first to understand the historical context in which it was written. In October 1874 William Gladstone, who until very recently had been prime minister, published an article which referred, in passing, to the 'effort to Romanise the Church and the people of England'. According to Gladstone, there was no longer any chance of that, now that 'no one can become her convert without renouncing his moral and mental freedom, and placing his civil loyalty and duty at the mercy of another', that is, the pope. Gladstone, of course, was referring to the definition of papal infallibility four years earlier at the First Vatican Council. Newman welcomed the outburst, which was understandable in view of the provocative Ultramontanism of the ultra-papal Cardinal Manning of Westminster, since it was possible for him to 'speak against Gladstone, while it would not be decent to speak against Manning'.[23]

During the next few weeks Newman tried to write something in answer to Gladstone, but without success. Then on 5 November, Guy Fawkes Day when the Catholic 'gunpowder plot' of 5 November 1605 was and is still commemorated in England with the burning of the pope in effigy, Gladstone provocatively published his pamphlet *The Vatican Decrees in their Bearing on Civil Allegiance: A Political Expostulation*. Gladstone thought (mistakenly) that the Pope had been behind the Irish Catholic bishops' opposition to his Irish University bill, which had failed to get through Parliament after Irish members had voted against it. His sense of grievance over this defeat in March 1873, which led to the fall of his government in February 1874, had been aggravated a few months later by the resignation of the Marquis of Ripon from the Cabinet, as a prelude to his becoming a Catholic.

---

[22] *GA* 73–5.
[23] Ian Ker, *John Henry Newman: A Biography* (Oxford: Clarendon Press, 1988), 679.

Gladstone's pamphlet, then, which was popular in tone and became a bestseller, was no mere academic exercise, and Newman saw immediately that it would have to be answered.

Newman completed his response to Gladstone on 21 December after a month's continuous writing, and the 'pamphlet', which was actually 150 pages of close print, was published on 14 January 1875. A few days later, his Oratorian confrere and close friend Ambrose St John published his translation of Bishop Fessler's *True and False Infallibility*; Fessler had been secretary-general at the First Vatican Council, and his book, which insisted on a strictly moderate interpretation of papal infallibility, had received the official approval of Pope Pius ıx. Along with Newman's *Letter to the Duke of Norfolk*, it was a significant blow to the extreme Ultramontanes. It was also of course in effect another response to Gladstone's own absurd exaggeration of the definition of papal infallibility, according to which a Catholic might be required to obey, say, an order by the pope to murder Queen Victoria.[24]

So that was the context in which Newman was writing: the question was whether Catholics could be loyal subjects or citizens of the state or whether they were now to all intents and purposes subjects in all respects, including political, to the papacy. But before looking at what Newman had to say in response, it is worth reminding ourselves of the contemporary secular context in which Newman's *Letter* is likely to be read and by which even Catholics are more than likely to be influenced.

The secular understanding of conscience, which has affected many Catholics, at least in the secularized West, is that conscience is something that is personal to oneself. Now, of course, it is perfectly true that, just as I can only think with *my own* mind and not somebody else's, so too I can only follow or not follow *my own* conscience, not somebody else's. But when people today speak of *my* conscience with the emphasis on *my*, they are thinking of the conscience as something a good deal more individual and personal than that. It is like speaking of *my* personality, *my* likes and dislikes. In authoritarian cultures and societies, of course, the opposite may happen: my conscience becomes the conscience of the state. And even in a secular, pluralist society the individual may equate law with morality: if the state

24   Ker, *John Henry Newman*, 680.

permits same-sex unions and outlaws any form of discrimination, then the citizen may feel that it is not homosexuality that is immoral but its condemnation. And it is certainly possible for Catholics, too, to *equate* their conscience with the teaching of the Church, which is not the same thing as conscientiously obeying the teaching of the Church. In his celebrated treatment of conscience in the *Letter to the Duke of Norfolk*, Newman follows the Catholic tradition by avoiding both extremes, that is, by emphasizing both the rights and the duties of conscience, for while conscience is personal to the person, conscience implies an authority outside the person. Newman begins by quoting St Thomas Aquinas's definition of the natural law as 'an impression of the Divine Light in us, a participation of the eternal law in the rational creature'. It is the human awareness of this law, however faulty this awareness may be in individual cases, that Newman defines as conscience:

> This law, as apprehended in the minds of individual men, is called 'conscience'; and though it may suffer refraction in passing into the intellectual medium of each, it is not therefore so affected as to lose its character of being the Divine Law, but still has, as such, the prerogative of commanding obedience.[25]

Conscience, therefore, does not belong to me like my personality, but nevertheless, even when it is in error, I have a duty to follow its dictates. The modern secular idea of conscience is that it is a 'creation of man', nothing more than 'a long-sighted selfishness' and—this is a characteristically penetrating observation by Newman—'a desire to be consistent with oneself'. Newman restates the traditional Catholic concept of conscience as sovereign but dependent on an external authority: 'Conscience is the aboriginal Vicar of Christ, a prophet in its informations, a monarch in its peremptoriness, a priest in its blessings and anathemas, and, even though the eternal priesthood throughout the Church would cease to be, in it the sacerdotal principle would remain and would have a sway.'[26] This 'stern monitor' has been replaced in a secularized society by a 'counterfeit', namely, 'the right of thinking, speaking, writing, acting, according to [one's] judgment or…humour, without any thought of God at all'—in other words, by what is nothing more than 'the right of self-will'. Conscience, then,

[25] *Diff*. ii.247.   [26] *Diff*. ii.247–9.

becomes simply 'the very right and freedom of conscience to dispense with conscience'.[27]

In *An Essay in Aid of a Grammar of Assent* Newman had spoken of conscience as 'a voice, or the echo of a voice, imperative and constraining, like no other dictate in the whole of our experience'.[28] The modification 'or the echo of a voice' is important because, although Newman maintains that 'the universal sense of right and wrong' is 'deeply lodged in the hearts of men', nevertheless he is well aware of the fragility of this sense, which 'is so delicate, so fitful, so easily puzzled, obscured, perverted, so subtle in its argumentative methods, so impressible by education, so biassed by pride and passion, so unsteady in its course', that paradoxically it is 'at once the highest of all teachers, yet the least luminous'. This is why the Church, whose 'mission is to proclaim the moral law, and to protect and strengthen' it, is 'the supply of an urgent demand'.[29]

Newman next turns to answer the objection that it is the existence of such an infallible authority that threatens the very sovereignty of conscience. He begins by laying down that 'conscience is not a judgment upon any speculative truth, any abstract doctrine, but bears immediately on conduct, on something to be done or not done'. Because conscience is concerned with what must be done or not done here and now, conscience 'cannot come into direct collision with the Church's or the Pope's infallibility; which is engaged on general propositions, and in the condemnation of particular and given errors'. Newman concludes:

> …conscience being a practical dictate, a collision is possible between it and the Pope's authority only when the Pope legislates, or gives particular orders, and the like. But a Pope is not infallible in his laws, nor in his commands, nor in his acts of state, nor in his administration, nor in his public policy.[30]

Newman then discusses the possibility of disobeying a papal edict or order, which he allows for, but for which he lays down very stringent conditions:

> If in a particular case conscience is to be taken as a sacred and sovereign monitor, its dictate, in order to prevail against the voice of the Pope, must follow upon serious thought, prayer, and all available means of

---

[27] *Diff.* ii.250.   [28] *GA* 74–5.   [29] *Diff.* ii.252–4.
[30] *Diff.* ii.256.

arriving at a right judgment on the matter in question. And further, obedience to the pope is what is called 'in possession'; that is, the *onus probandi* of establishing a case against him lies, as in all cases of exception, on the side of conscience. Unless a man is able to say to himself, as in the Presence of God, that he must not, and dare not, act upon the papal injunction, he is bound to obey it, and would commit a great sin in disobeying it.[31]

The frequently voiced claim, then, that Newman allowed for conscientious dissent from Church teachings is incorrect.[32] He did not: he only allowed for disobedience to orders. And the celebrated toast at the end of the *Letter to the Duke of Norfolk* concerns papal orders not teachings: 'Certainly, if I am obliged to bring religion into after-dinner toasts (which indeed does not seem quite the thing) I shall drink—to the Pope, if you please,—still, to Conscience first, and to the Pope afterwards.'[33] Newman was concerned with the charge that, by virtue of the definition of papal infallibility, Catholics could no longer be regarded as loyal law-abiding citizens since they were now subject to papal decrees and orders which they were bound to obey, however immoral.

Although it is true that Newman did, in accordance with Catholic tradition, hold that conscience is indeed supreme in the sense that it is—to use his own evocative phrase—'the aboriginal Vicar of Christ', with its obvious allusion to the pope who is traditionally called 'the Vicar of Christ', this famous toast was never intended by Newman to mean that a Catholic may be led by his conscience to dissent from Church teachings. Of course, he would have agreed with St Thomas Aquinas that a Catholic may, indeed should, follow an erroneous conscience even if it means leaving the Church. But a believing member of the Church has a conscientious duty to believe the teachings of the Church, not to pick and choose what to believe. The truth is that Newman was primarily concerned in the *Letter to the Duke of Norfolk*

---

[31] *Diff.* ii.257–8.

[32] See, for example, John R. Connolly, *John Henry Newman: A View of Catholic Faith for the New Millennium* (Lanham, MD: Rowman and Littlefield, 2005), who misinterprets Newman's acknowledgement that 'there are extreme cases in which Conscience may come into collision with the word of a Pope, and is to be followed in spite of that word' as applying to 'the noninfallible teachings of the pope' (p. 112), when actually 'the word' that Newman is talking about is a word of command not of teaching.

[33] *Diff.* ii.261.

to refute Gladstone's charge that the First Vatican Council's definition of papal infallibility deprived Catholics of their political freedom and made them subjects to a foreign power (the Holy See), and to show that the definition did nothing to subvert their patriotism or diminish their moral responsibility.

The idea that a Catholic may conscientiously dissent from the magisterium's moral teachings would have amazed Newman. The possibility never occurred to him. Writing before the ethical issues raised by advances in medical knowledge, he could write without batting an eyelid: 'So little does the Pope come into this whole system of moral theology by which (as by our conscience) our lives are regulated, that the weight of his hand upon us, as private men, is absolutely unappreciable.' Indeed, he adds, 'if my account be correct, I do not see what he takes away at all from our private conscience'. With blissful lack of prescience, he observes that 'the field of morals contains so little that is unknown and unexplored, in contrast with revelation and doctrinal fact...that it is difficult to say what portions of moral teaching in the course of 1800 years actually have proceeded from the Pope, or from the Church'.[34] Nevertheless, what Newman has to say about conscience and its relation to the teaching Church is still relevant. Whenever anyone uses their conscience to make a judgement about what should or should not be done here and now, that person, if he or she is making a conscientious judgement, will be applying whatever general moral principles they happen to hold. In the case of a Catholic, then, their conscience will be making a judgement in the light of the moral teachings of the Church. Now in the case of affirmative or positive teachings, such as the need to give generously to the needy from what one has, each person obviously has to make a conscientious judgement as to what that means for that person. No pope or bishop or priest can decide that; all they can do is to enunciate the general principle and urge that it be conscientiously put into practice. But what of negative teachings such as that it is always wrong to have an abortion, always wrong to wage indiscriminate warfare?[35] Might it not be argued that in the case of these absolute negative teachings that do not admit of exceptions, there is no room for the

---

[34] *Diff.* ii.229–32.

[35] For this objection, see John Finnis, 'Conscience in the *Letter to the Duke of Norfolk*', in Ian Ker and Alan G. Hill, eds, *Newman after a Hundred Years* (Oxford: Clarendon Press, 1990), 412–13.

individual Catholic conscience to make a practical judgement, and that the only judgement a Catholic can make in these circumstances is to follow an erroneous conscience and disobey the Church's teachings? In this case, there would indeed be a direct collision between the individual Catholic conscience and the Church's teaching authority *pace* Newman. But in such a case Newman would say that such an erroneous conscience was no longer a Catholic conscience, and because it rejected a general teaching of the Church such a conscience could indeed come into direct conflict with the Church.

What, however, of a faithful Catholic conscience in relation to absolute negative moral teachings? Has such a conscience any practical judgement to make except to obey the particular teaching? I think Newman would respond in two ways.

First, is it in fact possible so to frame such a teaching as to exclude all possible exceptions? To take a simple, obvious example, the commandment 'Thou shalt not kill' only applies to deliberate, wrongful killing. If I am driving in an urban area at the correct speed and a child jumps out in front of my car and is killed, I am not guilty of murder or of manslaughter. The fault, if there is any, lies with the child. Alternatively, the Church's tradition considers it permissible to kill deliberately in self-defence or in a just war, for such killing is deliberate but not wrongful. But what if we move from such a very general teaching to much more specific teachings, such as 'It is always wrong to wage warfare indiscriminately against whole cities' or 'It is always wrong to practise contraception'? Surely to these much more tightly framed teachings there can be no exceptions? But even here the conscientious Catholic has to use their conscience. A Catholic pilot on a bombing mission has to decide whether the instructions he has been given, if carried out, would constitute 'indiscriminate' warfare against a whole city. If the targets he is given are so vague or so indirectly connected with any military purpose, then he may conclude that that would be the case. On the other hand, if he considers the strategic targets are sufficiently defined and that it is possible to attack them without at the same time directly attacking the civilian population, he is justified in deciding that the action he had been ordered to carry out is one that would not bring his conscience into direct conflict with the Church's teaching. Here the question is: what constitutes *indiscriminate* warfare? The same is true of the Church's teaching on artificial contraception, which applies to the marital act not to cases where women are threatened with rape and where contraceptives may licitly be used provided they are not abortifacients. To take one more example, 'Thou shalt not steal' may sound a very straightforward absolute negative moral teaching, and yet the Catechism of the Catholic Church states unequivocally: 'There is no theft if... refusal [to give food to a penniless starving peasant, for example] is contrary to reason and the universal destination of goods.'[36] One could, of course, give many more instances of apparently absolute negative moral teachings that do admit of exceptions, or that do not apply in every apparent instance.

There is, I think, a second response that Newman would make to the objection. The teachings of the Church do not, as it were, speak for themselves, any more than the Bible does. They require interpretation, both as to their nature and their meaning. Not all teachings involve the exercise of infallibility. The degree of assent required of Catholics will vary with the degree of authority with which a particular teaching is invested. It also needs careful interpretation according to traditional theological norms. Newman was very emphatic that what he called the 'principle of minimizing'[37] should always operate so that no more than was strictly necessary should be asked of the faith of Catholics. This 'principle of minimizing' would take into account what Newman calls the 'intensely concrete character of the matters condemned' in negative teachings. In other words, as we have seen, not all acts of ostensible theft or contraception, for example, fall under the condemnation of the relevant absolute negative teachings. So-called affirmative teachings, on the other hand, do 'admit of exceptions in their actual application.'[38] Thus it is not a morally good action to give money to a penniless beggar on the streets if it aids and abets his addiction to drugs. Finally, Newman notes that an absolute negative moral teaching such as that on usury may have to be modified in the light of changing circumstances, without, of course, abandoning the essential principle which will require reinterpretation and reapplication in the new situation.

In conclusion, Newman's theology of the conscience and its relation to the teaching authority of the Church upholds the sovereignty, but not the autonomy, of the individual conscience. The conscience is sovereign only because it is the 'vicarius' of God, his substitute or delegate, but it is not autonomous because it is not a god but the servant

36 *Catechism of the Catholic Church*, 2408.   37 *Diff.* ii.332.
38 *Diff.* ii.334.

of God. The conscience is the spokesman not of the individual personality or temperament but of God. Since a Catholic believes that God speaks through his Church, the Catholic conscience hears the echo of God's voice in the teachings of the Church. If they are affirmative or positive, the individual conscience must judge as to their applicability in the particular case. But even when they are absolute and negative, the conscience must decide whether a particular action in fact falls within the scope of the teaching. Both positive and negative teachings require careful theological evaluation and interpretation in accordance with the theological norms and traditions of the Church.

4

The Constitution on the Liturgy was the first document to be completed by the Council; it was obviously also the document that had most effect on the life of the Church and the lives of Catholics. It would seem that Newman could have nothing to say about *Sacrosanctum Concilium* since this is the one document of the Council that he can scarcely be said to have anticipated in any way, as he never wrote about the liturgy and certainly was no forerunner of the liturgical movement of the twentieth century. However, there were and are unintended consequences of the promulgation of the Constitution on which he would certainly wish to comment.

The Constitution emphasizes at the outset that: 'the liturgy is the summit toward which the activity of the Church is directed; at the same time it is the fountain from which all her power flows' (art. 10). But almost immediately, the Constitution goes on to make it clear that: 'popular devotions of the Christian people are warmly commended' (art. 13). However, in the years after the Council not only were local popular devotions drastically downplayed or even abolished, but traditional devotions common to the whole Latin Church such as the rosary and stations of the cross were discouraged or even forbidden. More seriously still, eucharistic devotions were alleged to be 'medieval errors': ' "The Eucharistic Gifts are for eating, not for looking at"—these and similar slogans are all too familiar,' wrote the then Cardinal Ratzinger, in 2000. In fact, Ratzinger pointed out, they were authentic medieval developments, 'caused in part by the deepening of theological reflection, but still more important was the new experience of the saints, especially in the Franciscan movement and in the new evangelization undertaken by the Order of Preachers.[39]

All these unintended consequences, illegitimate developments of *Sacrosanctum Concilium*, would have horrified the Newman who wrote to a friend after his conversion: 'I could not have fancied the extreme, ineffable comfort of being in the same house with Him who cured the sick and taught His disciples...'. When he had been abroad, he 'did not know, or did not observe, the tabernacle Lamp—but now after tasting of the awful delight of worshipping God in His Temple, how unspeakably cold is the idea of a Temple without that Divine Presence! One is tempted to say what is the meaning, what is the use of it?'[40] It was the reservation of the Sacrament in the tabernacle in Catholic churches that more than anything else impressed and moved Newman after his conversion. To another close friend he wrote: 'I am writing next room to the Chapel—It is such an incomprehensible blessing to have Christ in bodily presence in one's house, within one's walls, as swallows up all other privileges... To know that He is close by—to be able again and again through the day to go in to Him... It is *the* place for intercession surely, where the Blessed Sacrament is.'[41] Arriving in Milan *en route* to Rome nearly a year after his conversion, he immediately noticed that he had another reason for preferring classical to gothic architecture—the high altar stood out more prominently as the focal point of the church, which meant that the tabernacle with the Blessed Sacrament enjoyed particular prominence: 'Nothing moves... but the distant glimmering Lamp which betokens the Presence of our Undying Life, hidden but ever working.' As he walked along the streets—it was late summer and the doors were thrown open because of the heat—he exclaimed that it was 'really most wonderful to see this Divine Presence looking out almost into the open streets from the various Churches.'[42] It is hard to imagine anything that would have dismayed Newman more than the relegation of the Blessed Sacrament from the high altar to a more or less obscure corner in countless churches after Vatican II. Like *Sacrosanctum Concilium*, Newman understood perfectly well that the Eucharist is 'the greatest action that can be on earth', as he put it in his

---

[39] Joseph Ratzinger, *The Spirit of the Liturgy*, tr. John Saward (San Francisco: Ignatius Press, 2000), 85, 89.
[40] *LD* xi.131.   [41] *LD* xi.129.   [42] *LD* xi.252.

first book after becoming a Catholic. But that same novel, *Loss and Gain*, ends with the convert hero kneeling before the tabernacle, having attended a litany and Benediction of the Blessed Sacrament, two traditional devotions that practically disappeared after the Council. He was, the author comments, kneeling before that 'Great Presence, which makes a Catholic Church different from every other place in the world'.[43]

Finally, *Sacrosanctum Concilium* called for the 'rite and formulas for the sacrament of penance' to be 'revised so that they give more luminous expression to both the nature and effect of the sacrament' (art. 72). But far from the sacrament of penance being renewed after the Council, in the years that followed the sacrament practically disappeared in large parts of the Western Church. There were no doubt a number of reasons for the demise of the sacrament, but there is no doubt that it was caused partly by the emphasis on social as opposed to individual sin that *Gaudium et Spes* was supposed to have encouraged, but partly also by an exaggerated idea of the Eucharist as the source and summit of the Christian life, which fostered the notion that the penitential rite at the beginning of Mass had removed the need for a special sacrament of penance.

This would have astonished and dismayed even the Anglican Newman, for whom the absence of the sacrament in the Church of England was nothing less than a pastoral disaster. In 1842 he wrote to John Keble: 'As to reminding my People about Confession, it is the most dreary and dismal thought which I have about my Parish that I dare do so little, or rather nothing. I have long thought it would hinder me ever taking another cure. Confession is the life of the Parochial charge—without it all is shallow...'. A year later, after resigning as vicar of the University Church, St Mary the Virgin, he wrote in similar vein to one of his sisters: 'If there were no other reason in the world, why I should not undertake a parochial cure in our Church, this alone would suffice for the future that there is no confession. I cannot understand how a clergyman can be answerable for souls, if souls are not admitted to him. There is *no real* cure of *souls* in our Church...'.[44]

[43] *LG* 328, 427.   [44] *LD* ix.175, 523.

5

The Declaration on the Relationship of the Church to Non-Christian Religions, *Nostra Aetate*, in its turn was misinterpreted as saying in effect that the Church was no longer to be seen 'as necessary for salvation', but simply as 'one of many places in which people could live a life of grace'.[45] In actuality, the Declaration was even less radical than Newman's theology of non-Christian religions. The document certainly affirmed that the Church 'rejects nothing which is true and holy' in other religions. And in consequence it called for the recognition of 'the spiritual and moral goods...as well as the values in their society and culture' of non-Christian religions (art. 2). But there was nothing in the least revolutionary about this: St Justin Martyr in the second century had attributed all truths in non-Christian religions to the Word of God who is, in the words of St John the Evangelist, 'the light of men' (Jn 1:1). Unfortunately, after the Council there was again a violent swing of the pendulum, in this case away from the common pre-conciliar attitude of missionaries that non-Christian religions were simply false and the work of the Devil to the totally untraditional and unorthodox idea that Christianity was merely one of many religions that lead people to God.

Newman would have rejected any kind of pluralist theology of religions, although he is more radical or liberal than *Nostra Aetate*. In the *Apologia* he records the great influence on him of the Alexandrian Fathers and how the 'broad philosophy of Clement and Origen carried [him] away'. This 'broad philosophy' included the idea that 'pagan literature, philosophy, and mythology, properly understood, were but a preparation for the Gospel', for the 'Greek poets and sages were in a certain sense prophets' and 'there had been in some sense a dispensation carried in favour of the Gentiles'.[46] In the *Arians* he had already acknowledged a 'doctrine of the Alexandrian school...which I shall call *the divinity of Traditionary Religion*'. According to the Bible itself, 'all knowledge of religion' is from God: 'There never was a time when God had not spoken to man, and told him to a certain extent his duty.' True, 'the Church of God ever has had, and the rest of mankind

45   Avery Cardinal Dulles, SJ, 'Nature, Mission, and Structure of the Church', in Matthew L. Lamb and Matthew Levering, eds, *Vatican II: Renewal within Tradition*, (New York: Oxford University Press, 2008), 25.
46   *Apo.* 36.

never have had, authoritative documents of truth, and appointed channels of communication' with God—'but all men have had more or less the guidance of Tradition, in addition to those internal notions of right and wrong which the Spirit has put into the heart of each individual'. Following St Clement, Newman feels free to call this 'vague and uncertain family of religious truths, originally from God, but sojourning without the sanctuary of miracle, or a definite home, as pilgrims up and down the world, and discernible and separable from the corrupt legends with which they are mixed, by the spiritual mind alone... the *Dispensation of Paganism*'. Moreover, Newman points out that 'Scripture gives us reason to believe that the traditions, thus originally delivered to mankind at large, have been secretly re-animated and enforced by new communications from the unseen world.'[47]

Just as Newman goes beyond the mere recognition of *Nostra Aetate* that good and truth are to be found in non-Christian religions, so too his advice to the Christian missionary anticipates but goes beyond Vatican II's Decree on the Missionary Activity of the Church, *Ad Gentes*, in recommending that the missionary should not only purify whatever is good and true in non-Christian religions but actually base his preaching of the gospel on such elements of good and truth. *Ad Gentes* merely affirms that 'whatever truth and grace are to be found among the nations, as a sort of secret presence of God, [missionary] activity frees from all taint of evil and restores to Christ its maker...And so, whatever good is found to be sown in the hearts and minds of men, or in the rites and cultures peculiar to various people, is not lost...it is healed, ennobled, and perfected...' (art. 9). But the Anglican Newman doesn't hesitate to advise the Christian missionary:

> Believing God's hand to be in every system, so far forth as it is true (though Scripture alone is the depositary of His unadulterated and complete revelation), he will, after St. Paul's manner, seek some points in the existing superstitions as the basis of his own instructions, instead of indiscriminately condemning and discarding the whole assemblage of heathen opinions and practices... And while he strenuously opposes all that is idolatrous, immoral, and profane, in their creed, he will profess to be leading them on to perfection, and to be recovering and purifying, rather than reversing the essential principles of their belief.[48]

---

[47] *Ari.* 79–81.   [48] *Ari.* 83–4.

Newman is not only explicit that the good and true elements in non-Christian religions come from God, whose 'Revelation, properly speaking, is an universal, not a local gift',[49] but he is also clear that 'God uses the rites and customs of pagan religions to realize His salvific will',[50] writing in *The Idea of a University*:

> He introduces Himself, he all but concurs...in the issues of unbelief, superstition, and false worship, and He changes the character of acts by His overruling operation. He condescends, though He gives no sanction, to the altars and shrines of imposture, and He makes His own fiat the substitute for its sorceries. He speaks amid the incantations of Balaam, raises Samuel's spirit in the witch's cavern, prophesies of the Messias by the tongue of the Sibyl...and baptizes by the hand of the misbeliever.[51]

This again goes beyond what the Council teaches, and raises 'a possibility which Vatican II never considered, namely that the mediation of the Church might not be essential for the salvation of every man and woman. The Second Vatican Council appears to teach that the Church is always at least implicated in the salvific process realized in Christ...'.[52] Although God instituted the sacraments as the normal means of salvation, Newman wrote in a sermon of 1832, 'He can sustain our immortality without the Christian sacraments, as He sustained Abraham and the other saints of old time.'[53] And, if 'just men existed before Christ came', he wondered as a Catholic, why should there should not be 'just men among the *heathen*'?[54] Indeed, he pointed out, 'it does not follow, because there is no Church but one, which has the Evangelical gifts and privileges to bestow, that therefore no one can be saved without the intervention of that one Church.'[55] Yet, radical as Newman was in comparison with Vatican II, he was 'no pluralist': 'His theology of religions is radically incarnational. "All the providences of God centre" in Christ...His salvific work "is the sole Meritorious Cause, the sole Source of spiritual blessing to our guilty race".'[56] And although he held that it is possible to be saved outside

---

[49]   *Ari.* 80.
[50]   Terrence Merrigan, 'The Anthropology of Conversion: Newman and the Contemporary Theology of Religions', in Ian Ker, ed., *Newman and Conversion* (Edinburgh: T & T Clark, 1997), 130.
[51]   *Idea* 68.   [52]   Merrigan, 'The Anthropology of Conversion', 131.
[53]   *PS* i.275.   [54]   *SN* 328.   [55]   *Diff.* ii.335.
[56]   Merrigan, 'The Anthropology of Conversion', 131, citing *GA* 43 and *PS* ii.304.

His Church, nevertheless he was insistent that 'there is no other Communion or Polity which has the promises'.[57] Newman would have certainly concurred with the teaching of *Lumen Gentium* that the Church is 'the universal sacrament of salvation' (art. 48), but he also maintained that the Catholic doctrine that ' "Out of the Church is no salvation"... meant, there is no religious body but one in which *is* salvation'—not that there is no 'grace external to the Church'.[58]

[57] *LD* xxvi.364.   [58] *LD* xxx.33.

6

Secularization and the New Evangelization

1

It is time now to return to the subject of evangelization, a topic that was not an explicit theme of the Second Vatican Council apart from the decree on foreign missions. The evangelization to which Pope Paul VI called the Church in 1975[1] was not so much the evangelization of pagans or non-Christians as what Pope John Paul II was to call the 'new evangelization' or the 're-evangelization' of secularized post-Christians.[2] This call for a 'new evangelization' led Pope Benedict XVI in 2010 to establish a Pontifical Council for the Promotion of the New Evangelization. And in 2013 his successor, Pope Francis, devoted his first major teaching document, the Apostolic Exhortation *Evangelii Gaudium*, to the subject of evangelization, the topic of the previous year's synod of bishops (his encyclical *Lumen Fidei*, issued earlier in the year to close the 'Year of Faith' that his predecessor had called for the year previously, was largely written by the previous pope, as Francis acknowledged[3]). It is, then, this need for a 'new evangelization' that has to a large extent superseded the preoccupations of the Second Vatican Council and the immediate post-conciliar period. Does this mean that Newman, 'the Father of the Second Vatican Council', is less relevant to the contemporary Church than he was? In so far as the new ecclesial communities and movements are vital to this 'new evangelization', clearly this is not the case, as we saw in Chapter 3.[4] But does Newman have anything to contribute apart from that?

---

[1] See Chapter 3, section 3, p. 81.   [2] *Redemptoris Missio* (1990), 3, 33.
[3] *Lumen Fidei*, art. 7.   [4] See Chapter 3, section 3, pp. 92–4, 100–2, 106.

In a sermon of 1873 at the opening of a new seminary, Newman warned the seminarians that

> the trials which lie before us are such as would appal and make dizzy even such courageous hearts as St. Athanasius, St. Gregory i, or St. Gregory vii. And they would confess that, dark as the prospect of their own day was to them severally, ours has a darkness different in kind from any that has been before it.

The phenomenon that Newman was referring to is what today we would call 'secularization'. Christianity had 'never yet had experience of a world simply irreligious'[5] till the nineteenth century. The Church had had plenty of experience of dealing with pagans, but not of a world where the supernatural seemed to have disappeared from human consciousness, a world where, Newman warned presciently, Catholics were likely to be 'regarded as...the enemies...of civil liberty and of national progress'.[6]

It would be natural to assume that Newman would recommend the Christian apologist to approach the secular post-Christian with the argument from conscience. After all, in the *Grammar of Assent* he had called conscience the 'great internal teacher of religion'. It was the great teacher because it was 'a personal guide, and I use it because I must use myself', and because therefore it was 'nearer to me than any other means of knowledge'. And if he had to 'prove the Being of a God', it would be in conscience that he would 'look for the proof of it'.

> As from a multitude of instinctive perceptions...of something beyond the senses, we generalize the notion of an external world, and then picture that world in and according to those particular phenomena from which we started, so from the perceptive power which identifies the intimations of conscience with the reverberations or echoes (so to say) of an external admonition, we proceed on to the notion of a Supreme Ruler and Judge, and then again we image Him and His attributes in those recurring intimations, out of which, as mental phenomena, our recognition of His existence was originally gained.[7]

Similarly, in the *Apologia* Newman acknowledges, 'Were it not for this voice, speaking so clearly in my conscience and my heart, I should

---

[5]   CS 121, 123.
[6]   CS 128. See Owen Chadwick, *The Secularization of the European Mind in the Nineteenth Century* (Cambridge: Cambridge University Press, 1975).
[7]   GA 251, 72.

be an atheist, or a pantheist, or a polytheist when I looked into the world.'[8]

It is, then, remarkable that in the one work where Newman depicts a conversion to Christianity, conscience plays no role at all. The heroine of his novel *Callista* is a Greek pagan, or rather post-pagan, girl, who, with her brother, Ariosto, has come to Sicca in North Africa to work as an artist for a merchant called Jucundus, who is 'warmly attached to the reigning paganism' and who 'drove a thriving trade in idols, large and small, amulets, and the like'. However, neither brother nor sister had any 'special attachment' to paganism or any other religion. Indeed, Callista sounds very like the typical Victorian who has lost their faith. In Greece she had worshipped Apollo, the god of light and the sun:

> 'At home I used to lie awake at night longing for the morning, and crying out for the god of day. It was like choice wine to me, a cup of Chian, the first streaks of the Aurora, and I could hardly bear his bright coming, when he came to me like Semele, for rapture. How gloriously did he shoot over the hills! And then anon he rested awhile on the snowy summit of Olympus, as in some luminous shrine, gladdening the Phrygian plain. Fair, bright-haired god! thou art my worship, if Callista worships aught: but somehow I worship nothing now. I am weary.'

Feeling 'a weariness in all things,'[9] Callista would have had some understanding of how Matthew Arnold felt when he spoke of the 'melancholy, long, withdrawing roar' of the 'Sea of Faith'.[10]

Callista has a suitor, Agellius, the nephew of Jucundus, who was baptized as a small boy. He has retained his faith but has no chance of practising it properly as the Church has virtually ceased to exist in Sicca. Callista has had contact with Christianity through a slave of hers called Chione, who exemplifies the importance of what Newman called 'personal influence' in evangelizing[11]: 'She was unlike any one I have seen before or since; she cared for nothing, yet was not morose or peevish or hard-hearted.' Instead of pressing his suit, Callista wishes that Agellius could have taught her 'more of that strange strength which my nature needs, and which she [Chione] told me she possessed'. So bitterly disappointed is she that he has made love

---

[8] *Apo.* 216–17.   [9] *Call.* 21, 95, 117–18.
[10] 'Dover Beach', ll.21, 25.
[11] See 'Personal Influence, the Means of Propagating the Truth', *US* 75–98; cf. *Apo.* 47.

to her instead of speaking to her of his God that she cries out in her frustration: 'So the religion of Chione is a dream...I had hoped it was a reality. All things again are vanity; I had hoped there was something somewhere more than I could see; but there is nothing.' Now a reader of the *Grammar of Assent* might well assume that Callista is suffering from a troubled conscience, a sense of sin, and looking for possible forgiveness from the God of the Christians. But in fact, conscience is not the issue, rather something quite different:

> 'Here am I a living, breathing woman, with an over-flowing heart, with keen affections, with a yearning after some object which may possess me. I cannot exist without something to rest upon. I cannot fall back upon that drear, forlorn state, which philosophers call wisdom, and moralists call virtue...I must have something to love; love is my life...You have thrown me back upon my dreary, dismal self...'

Poor Agellius belatedly assures Callista, who wanted to hear about his God and not about his love, that the Christian God 'satisfies every affection of the heart'.[12]

When Callista meets the priest Caecilius, in reality St Cyprian the Bishop of Carthage, he asks her if she is not unhappy after she objects to the Christian doctrine of Hell, and when she agrees that she is he suggests that she will only become the more unhappy the longer she lives: 'At the end of two hundred years you would be too miserable even for your worst enemy to rejoice in it.' In fact, though, she will die:

> 'Perhaps you will tell me that you will then cease to be. I don't believe you think so. I may take for granted that you think with me, and with the multitude of men, that you will still live, that you will still be *you*. You will still be the same being, but deprived of those outward stays and reliefs and solaces, which, such as they are, you now enjoy. You will be yourself, shut up in yourself.'

Caecilius then argues that, since 'the soul always needs external objects to rest upon' and since 'it has no prospect of any such when it leaves this visible scene', then 'there is nothing irrational in the notion of an eternal Tartarus', for 'the hunger and thirst, the gnawing of the heart' will be 'as keen and piercing as a flame'. Having answered Callista's objection to the idea of Hell by explaining that it consists in just the kind of self-imprisonment that Callista seeks to escape from,

---

[12] *Call.* 126, 130–3.

he then in the same way challenges her to respond to the case for Christianity, which he presents precisely as offering liberation from the prison of the self:

> '...if you have needs, desires, aims, aspirations, all of which demand an Object, and imply, by their very existence, that such an Object does exist also; and if nothing here does satisfy them, and if there be a message which professes to come from that Object, of whom you already have the presentiment, and to teach you about Him, and to bring the remedy you crave; and if those who try that remedy say with one voice that the remedy answers; are you not bound, Callista, at least to look that way...?'

Callista demands to know what this 'remedy' is, this 'Object', this 'love'. And Caecilius gives what Newman presumably thought was the best apologetic for the 'new evangelization', that is the evangelization of secular as opposed to pagan man, namely, a response to secular man's sense of unfulfilment and desire for happiness:

> 'Every man is in that state which you confess of yourself. We have no love for Him who alone lasts. We love those things which do not last, but come to an end. Things being thus, He whom we ought to love has determined to win us back to Him. With this object He has come into His own world, in the form of one of us men. And in that human form He opens His arms and woos us to return to Him, our Maker. This is our Worship, this is our Love, Callista.'

And then Callista realizes that, if this is true, then her own 'notion of the First and only Fair', which she had learned from Greek philosophy, has become 'embodied in a substance'—the Word has become flesh.[13]

As time passed, the more Callista 'thought over what she heard of Christianity, the more she was drawn to it, and the more it approved itself to her whole soul, and the more it seemed to respond to all her needs and aspirations, and the more intimate was her presentiment that it was true'. The more she thought about it, 'the more it seemed (unlike the mythology or the philosophy of her country, or the political religion of Rome) to have an external reality and substance, which deprived objections to it of their power, and showed them to be at best but difficulties and perplexities'. What impressed her was that all the three Christians she had met, Chione, Agellius, and Caecilius, had

---

[13] *Call.* 217–22.

'made it [Christianity] to consist in the intimate Divine Presence in the heart':

> It was the friendship or mutual love of person with person. Here was the very teaching which already was so urgently demanded both by her reason and her heart, which she found nowhere else; which she found existing one and the same in a female slave, in a country youth, in a learned priest.[14]

Conscience, then, receives no mention at all in the first stage of Callista's conversion. Only when she has become fully convinced of the existence of a personal God, does she declare in front of her dismayed brother:

> 'I feel that God within my heart. I feel myself in His presence. He says to me, "Do this: don't do that." You may tell me that this dictate is a mere law of my nature, as it is to joy or to grieve. I cannot understand this. No, it is the echo of a person speaking to me. Nothing shall persuade me that it does not ultimately proceed from a person speaking to me. Nothing shall persuade me that it does not ultimately proceed from a person external to me. It carries with it its proof of its divine origin. My nature feels towards it as towards a person. When I obey it, I feel a satisfaction; when I disobey, a soreness—just like that which I feel in pleasing or offending some revered friend.'

The 'echo' she hears 'implies a voice; a voice a speaker. That speaker I love and I fear.'[15]

Presumably, when Newman wrote in the *Grammar of Assent* that he would prove the existence of God on the basis of conscience, he was speaking of *philosophical* proof. But in a real life situation as he depicts it in a novel, conscience *in the first place* plays no perceptible role at all. Here it is not the dictates of conscience but the demands of the heart that are crucial. The two are juxtaposed in that sentence from the *Apologia* already quoted,[16] where Newman says, 'Were it not for this voice, speaking so clearly in my conscience and my heart, I should be an atheist...'.[17]

Callista is converted to the God of Christianity for the reason that Newman sets out in one of his finest Anglican sermons, 'The Thought of God, the Stay of the Soul' (1837), and it has nothing to do primarily with conscience but with the fact that, as Newman puts it in another

---

[14] *Call.* 292–3.   [15] *Call.* 314–15.   [16] See section 1, pp. 133–4.
[17] *Apo.* 216.

Anglican sermon, 'the Gospel...supplies our very need.'[18] Without a personal God, Newman maintains, a person 'has faculties and affections without a ruling principle, object, or purpose'. Arguing that 'the happiness of the soul consists in the exercise of the affections', then, Newman contends, 'here is at once a reason for saying that the thought of God, and nothing short of it, is the happiness of man', since 'the affections require a something more vast and more enduring than anything created'.[19] We are reminded of St Augustine's famous words, 'our hearts are restless till they rest in you',[20] when we read the equivalent in Newman: 'He alone is sufficient for the heart who made it.' Other human beings cannot satisfy us, partly because they are transient and unreliable in their frailty: 'our hearts require something more permanent and uniform than man can be...Do not all men die? Are they not taken from us? Are they not as uncertain as the grass of the field?' But even apart from this, 'there is another reason why God alone is the happiness of our souls', as Newman explains:

> the contemplation of Him, and nothing but it, is able fully to open and relieve the mind, to unlock, occupy, and fix our affections. We may indeed love things created with great intenseness, but such affection, when disjoined from the love of the Creator, is like a stream running in a narrow channel, impetuous, vehement, turbid. The heart runs out, as it were, only at one door; it is not an expanding of the whole man. Created natures cannot open us, or elicit the ten thousand mental senses which belong to us, and through which we really live. None but the presence of our Maker can enter us; for to none besides can the whole heart in all its thoughts and feelings be unlocked and subjected.

The love and sympathy of those closest to us cannot rival the intimacy we can enjoy with God alone:

> It is this feeling of simple and absolute confidence and communion, which soothes and satisfies those to whom it is vouchsafed. We know that even our dearest friends enter into us but partially, and hold intercourse with us only at times; whereas the consciousness of a perfect and enduring Presence, and it alone, keeps the heart open.

It is only ultimately God, then, who can liberate the human heart from the prison of the self:

---

[18] *PS* iii.124.   [19] *PS* v.314–16.   [20] *Confessions*, I.1.

Withdraw the Object on which it rests, and it will relapse again into its state of confinement and constraint; and in proportion as it is limited, either to certain seasons or to certain affections, the heart is straightened and distressed. If it be not over bold to say it, He who is infinite can alone be its measure; He alone can answer to the mysterious assemblage of feelings and thoughts which it has within it.

That is why true happiness depends on belief in God, as otherwise, 'We are pent up within ourselves, and are therefore miserable.'

[W]e need a relief to our hearts, that they may be dark and sullen no longer, or that they may not go on feeding upon themselves; we need to escape from ourselves to something beyond; and much as we may wish it otherwise, and may try to make idols to ourselves, nothing short of God's presence is our true refuge; everything else is either a mockery, or but an expedient useful for its season or in its measure.

And so it is not in the first place the voice of conscience that demands the existence of a personal God, but rather it is the self seeking liberation from its self-imprisonment in the only object external to itself which can offer true personal fulfilment, for a person cannot properly 'live without an object': either, then, we live in the unhappiness of the prison of our own self—or we try vainly to find self-fulfilment in other ephemeral people or things. As Newman puts it in a particularly powerful passage, in the latter case a person

fancies that he is sufficient for himself; or he supposes that knowledge is sufficient for his happiness; or that exertion, or that the good opinion of others, or (what is called) fame, or that the comforts and luxuries of wealth, are sufficient for him. What a truly wretched state is that coldness and dryness of soul, in which so many live and die. Many a great man, many a peasant, many a busy man, lives and dies with closed heart, with affections undeveloped and unexercised. You see the poor man, passing day after day, Sunday after Sunday, year after year, without a thought in his mind, to appearance almost like a stone. You see the educated man, full of thought, full of intelligence, full of action, but still with a stone heart, as cold and dead as regards his affections, as if he were the poor ignorant countryman. You see others, with warm affections, perhaps, for their families, with benevolent feelings towards their fellow-men, yet stopping there; centring their hearts on what is sure to fail them, as being perishable. Life passes, riches fly away, popularity is fickle, the senses decay, the world changes, friends die. One alone is constant; One alone is true to us; One alone can be true; One alone can be all things to us; One alone can supply our needs; One alone can train us up to our full perfection; One alone can give a meaning to our complex and intricate nature; One alone can give us tune and harmony; One alone can form and possess us.[21]

In *Callista* the apologetic approach of this great sermon is simply given dramatic actuality. Faced with the unbelief of secular man, Newman unabashedly appeals to the universal human desire for happiness and self-fulfilment, emphasizing not the dictates of conscience but the demands of self-interest, the need to respond to the 'affections and aspirations pent up within' the human heart.[22] Nevertheless the human 'need' that the gospel 'supplies' also, of course, includes the need to respond to the promptings of conscience, and, just as conscience is not excluded (although not given first place) in *Callista*, so too elsewhere in another sermon Newman includes conscience in his account of the human 'need' that the gospel 'supplies':

There is a voice within us, which assures us that there is something higher than earth. We cannot analyze, define, contemplate what it is that thus whispers to us. It has no shape or material form. There is that in our hearts which prompts us to religion, and which condemns and chastises sin. And this yearning of our nature is met and sustained, it finds an object to rest upon, when it hears of the existence of an All-powerful, All-gracious Creator.[23]

For Newman the existence of a personal God is involved in the very existence of the self. It is when we understand the true nature and needs of the human person that we understand that there must be a personal God. This was what Newman himself felt in the depths of his own being when in his youth he rested 'in the thought of two and two only absolute and luminously self-evident beings, myself and my Creator'.[24] However, in one of his Anglican sermons he recognized that it was more natural for fallen human beings to 'look off from self to the things around us, and forget ourselves in them'. The self has either to turn in on itself or to seek some external reality to rest in, and fallen human beings naturally incline to 'depending for support on the reeds which are no stay'. And Newman powerfully conveys a sense of the vanity of this transitory world:

…its changes are so many, so sudden, so silent, so continual. It never leaves changing; it goes on to change, till we are quite sick at heart:—then

---

[21] *PS* v.316–19, 324–6.   [22] *PS* iii.124.   [23] *PS* vi.339–40.
[24] *Apo.* 18.

it is that our reliance on it is broken. It is plain we cannot continue to depend on it, unless we keep pace with it, and go on changing too; but this we cannot do. We feel that, while it changes, we are one and the same...and we begin, by degrees, to perceive that there are but two beings in the whole universe, our own soul, and the God who made it.

For when disillusion with the world overcomes us, as it did Callista, then we come to realize that 'We still crave for something, we do not well know what; but we are sure it is something which the world has not given us.'[25]

Newman has been criticized for 'concentrating his energies so exclusively on one aspect of our experience, our awareness of moral obligation', for 'a unilateral concentration on moral experience', that is, 'our experience of conscience'.[26] But the criticism can only apply to his philosophical writings. Neither in his novel of conversion nor in his preaching does he stress the argument from conscience, but rather that self-fulfilment that human nature demands: the need to love and to be loved, the need for a mutual sympathy that cannot be broken and that is all-satisfying: 'the soul of man is made for the contemplation of its Maker; and...nothing short of that high contemplation is its happiness'. And 'if we are allowed to find that real and most sacred Object on which our heart may fix itself, a fullness of peace will follow, which nothing but it can give'.[27]

2

Callista's conversion to Christianity is, however, not quite complete. The personal God of Christianity alone seemed to offer her meaning and fulfilment. But she was still 'in the midway region of inquiry', which her author tells us from his own experience,[28] 'as surely takes time to pass over...as it takes time to walk from place to place': 'To see that heathenism is false,—to see that Christianity is true,—are two acts and involve two processes.' The second stage of her conversion takes place when she reads a manuscript copy of St Luke's Gospel

---

[25] *PS* i.19–20.
[26] Aidan Nichols, OP, *A Grammar of Consent: The Existence of God in Christian Tradition* (Edinburgh: T & T Clark, 1991), 1, 19, 35.
[27] *PS* v.315, 321.   [28] See *Apo.* 155–6.

that Caecilius had entrusted her with, remembering how he had said,
'Here you will see who it is we love.'

> Here was that to which her intellect tended, though that intellect could
> not frame it. It could approve and acknowledge, when set before it, what
> it could not originate. Here was He who spoke to her in her conscience;
> whose Voice she heard, whose Person she was seeking for... That image
> sank deep into her; she felt it to be a reality.[29]

Years after publishing the novel, Newman expressed his disappoint-
ment that Catholics had never 'done justice to the book; they read it
as a mere story book'. In fact, he thought, 'Protestants are more likely
to gain something from it.'[30] He surely had in mind the whole genera-
tions of Victorian Protestants who, like Matthew Arnold, had abandoned the Christian faith, who were no longer in fact Protestants but
secularized post-Christians, to whom he felt the book had something
important to say. And the absence of any reference to the novel in
contemporary discussions of Newman's philosophy of religion shows
that the neglect of *Callista* as a serious work of apologetics continues
to this day.[31]

As in *Callista*, so too in the *Grammar of Assent* Newman was to
maintain that Christianity of all the religions in the world alone 'tends
to fulfil' human 'aspirations, needs', for it is Jesus Christ who 'fulfils
the one great need of human nature, the Healer of its wounds, the
Physician of the soul'.[32] And the way we encounter Christ is the way
that Callista met him—through reading the Gospels. The reason,
Newman thought, as we saw earlier,[33] why so many Catholics abandon
their religion is because 'They have not impressed upon their hearts
the life of our Lord and Saviour as given us in the Evangelists', they do
not believe 'with the heart', and lack 'a faith founded in a personal love

---

[29]   *Call.* 317, 326.   [30]   *LD* xxvi.130.

[31]   There is no reference to *Callista* or the argument from the heart in the discussion
of Newman in Avery Cardinal Dulles, *A History of Apologetics* (Eugene, Oregon: Wipf
and Stock, 1999), 245–50. One modern literary critic, who can scarcely have read the
novel, dismisses it as mere pious saccharine hagiography: '*Callista* even might be said
to resemble the saint's life read by the mother to her little boy in [Graham Greene's]
The Power and the Glory' (Roger Sharrock, 'Newman's Poetry', in Ian Ker and Alan G.
Hill, eds, *Newman after a Hundred Years* (Oxford: Clarendon Press, 1990), 45).

[32]   *GA* 277, 299. The following section is an edited and enlarged version of Chapter 3,
'The Person of Jesus Christ', in my *Healing the Wound of Humanity: The Spirituality of
John Henry Newman* (London: Darton, Longman and Todd, 1993), 23–42.

[33]   See Chapter 2, section 3, p. 51.

for the Object of Faith.[34] To the question, how do we learn to love God, he answered simply in one of his Catholic sermon notes, 'By reading of our Lord in the Gospels.'[35] But, of course, Newman also knew that we encounter Christ, albeit less directly, through the Church, through Christians. For it was 'that wonderful unity of sentiment and belief in persons so dissimilar from each other' as Chione, Agellius, and Caecilius, 'so distinct in their circumstances, so independent in their testimony, which recommended to [Callista] the doctrine which they were so unanimous in teaching'.[36]

Newman was clear that his own preaching must be above all else 'real' in bringing out the 'reality' of the Gospels.[37] He wanted to depict Christ not in an 'unreal way—as a mere idea or vision', but as 'Scripture has set Him before us in His actual sojourn on earth, in His gestures, words, and deeds'. Instead of using of using 'vague statements about His love, His willingness to receive the sinner, His imparting repentance and spiritual aid, and the like', his aim as a preacher was to present 'Christ as manifested in the Gospels, the Christ who exists therein, external to our own imaginings…really a living being'.[38]

Because of the 'high' Christology that Newman took from the Alexandrian Fathers, he has been criticized for paying only notional attention to the humanity of Christ.[39] But certainly in his preaching it was the human figure of Christ in the Gospels that Newman was anxious to depict in all its humanity. In one of his posthumously published meditations he is insistent that Jesus was actually *more* human than any human being who has ever lived:

> Thou camest not only a perfect man, but as proper man; not formed anew out of earth, not with the spiritual body which Thou now hast, but in that very flesh which had fallen in Adam, and with all our infirmities, all our feelings and sympathies, sin excepted….
>
> O dearest Lord, Thou art more fully man than the holy Baptist, than St. John, Apostle and Evangelist, than Thy own sweet Mother. As in Divine knowledge of me Thou are beyond them all, so also in experience and personal knowledge of my nature. Thou art my elder brother.[40]

---

[34] *LD* xxvi.87.   [35] *SN* 125.   [36] *Call.* 292–3.   [37] *LD* v.327.
[38] *PS* iii.130–1.
[39] For a response, see Roderick Strange, 'Newman and the Mystery of Christ', in Ian Ker and Alan G. Hill, eds, *Newman after a Hundred Years* (Oxford: Clarendon Press, 1990), 323–36.
[40] *MD* 360.

Although no one was more insistent on the divinity of Christ against the liberal Protestant tendency to downplay it, no one was more anxious to emphasize the reality of the Incarnation, whereby Jesus Christ took to himself human nature, not 'as something distinct and separate from Himself, but as simply, absolutely, eternally His, so as to be included by us in the very thought of Him'.[41] Newman thought that, if there was a ' "leading idea" ... of Christianity', then the Incarnation was 'the central aspect of Christianity, out of which the three main aspects of its teaching take their rise, the sacramental, the hierarchical, and the ascetic'. It is true that he immediately modifies this by adding, 'But one aspect of Revelation must not be allowed to exclude or to obscure another.' However, later in the *Essay on the Development of Christian Doctrine*, he writes, cautiously again, 'For the convenience of arrangement, I will consider the Incarnation as the central truth of the gospel, and the source whence we are to draw our principles.'[42]

The historian James Anthony Froude has left a record of the power with which Newman made real for his congregation the person of Christ. At the height of the Oxford Movement Froude was present in the University Church of St Mary the Virgin when Newman preached 'The Incarnate Son, a Sufferer and Sacrifice' (1836). Froude's account of what Newman actually said is not accurate, but it is still worth quoting to show the effect of Newman's preaching. Having, according to Froude, 'described closely some of the incidents of our Lord's passion', Newman then 'paused'.

> For a few minutes there was a breathless silence. Then, in a low, clear voice, of which the faintest vibration was audible in the farthest corner of St Mary's, he said, 'Now, I bid you recollect that He to whom these things were done was Almighty God.' It was as if an electric stroke had gone through the church, as if every person present understood for the first time the meaning of what he had all his life been saying. I suppose it was an epoch in the mental history of more than one of my Oxford contemporaries.[43]

In actual fact the dramatic moment came after Newman had been insisting that God did suffer on the cross not in his divine but in his human nature—'God the Son suffered *in* that human nature which He had taken to Himself and made His own':

---

[41]   *MD* 360, 412.   [42]   *Dev.* 35–6, 324.
[43]   James Anthony Froude, *Short Studies on Great Subjects*, fourth series (New York: Charles Scribner's Sons, 1910), 188.

Think of this, all ye light-hearted, and consider whether with this thought you can read the last chapters of the four Gospels without fear and trembling. For instance; 'When He had thus spoken, one of the officers which stood by struck Jesus with the palm of his hand, saying, Answerest thou the high priest so?' The words must be said, though I hardly dare say them,—that officer lifted up his hand against God the Son. This is not a figurative way of speaking, or a rhetorical form of words, or a harsh, extreme, and unadvisable statement; it is a literal and simple truth, it is a great Catholic dogma.[44]

It was all very well to speak in a general kind of way about the Incarnation, but for Newman to make the Incarnation *real* as opposed to merely *notional*, to use the famous distinction of the *Grammar of Assent*, it was necessary to draw out the concrete implications: it was because God had become man in the form of a particular Jew living in a particular place at a particular time that it was possible for a man actually to strike his Creator.

In perhaps the best of his Catholic sermons, 'Mental Sufferings of our Lord in His Passion' (1849), Newman asks: if Jesus was really and truly God incarnate, then what must have been the real nature of his suffering on the Cross? And he answers first by pointing out that since Jesus was truly human he had a soul as well as a body. His suffering was therefore also completely human since human pain is not just physical but also spiritual: 'there is no real pain, though there may be apparent suffering, when there is no kind of inward sensibility or spirit to be the seat of it'. Animals cannot feel pain in the same way that human beings do 'because they cannot reflect on what they feel; they have no advertence or direct consciousness of their sufferings. This is it that makes pain so trying, viz., that we cannot help thinking of it, while we suffer it.' This is why human beings in intense agony feel

that they have borne *as much* as they can bear; as if the continuance and not the intenseness was what made it too much for them. What does this mean, but that the memory of the foregoing moments of pain acts upon and (as it were) edges the pain that succeeds? If the third or fourth or twentieth moment of pain could be taken by itself, if the succession of the moments that preceded it could be forgotten, it would be no more than the first moment, as bearable as the first (taking away the shock which accompanies the first); but what makes it unbearable is, that it *is* the twentieth... It is the intellectual comprehension of pain, as a whole

[44] *PS* vi.73.

diffused through successive moments, which gives it its special power and keenness, and it is the soul only, which a brute has not, which is capable of that comprehension.

Newman now applies his analogy to the suffering of Christ:

> Do you recollect their offering Him wine mingled with myrrh, when He was on the point of being crucified? He would not drink of it; why? Because such a potion would have stupefied His mind, and He was bent on bearing the pain in all its bitterness... He did not turn away His face from the suffering; He confronted it, or, as I may say, He breasted it that every particular portion of it might make its due impression on Him. And as men are superior to brute animals, and are affected by pain more than they, by reason of the mind within them, which gives a substance to pain, such as it cannot have in the instance of brutes; so, in like manner, our Lord felt pain of the body, with an advertence and a consciousness, and therefore with a keenness and intensity, and with a unity of perception, which none of us can possibly fathom or compass, because His soul was so absolutely in His power, so simply free from the influence of distractions, so fully directed *upon* the pain, so utterly surrendered, so simply subjected to the suffering. And thus He may truly be said to have suffered the whole of His passion in every moment of it.[45]

Newman may seem practically to deny the humanity of Christ when he says that Christ was in complete control of his passion: 'The soul of other men is subjected to its own wishes, feelings, impulses, passions, perturbations; His soul was subjected simply to His eternal and Divine personality. Nothing happened to His soul by chance, or on a sudden; He never was taken by surprise, nothing affected Him without His willing beforehand that it should affect Him.' But what is so striking is that the conclusion Newman draws from the fully voluntary nature of Christ's suffering is that Christ suffered *in his humanity* far more than he would have done if had been *only* a human being. In other words, instead of his divinity diminishing his pain on the Cross, it actually caused a thoroughly human pain utterly in excess of anything we can conceive of. To the objection that Christ could not have suffered as much as an ordinary human being would if he was the Son of God and knew he was, Newman's reply is that the opposite is true, namely that Christ suffered so much in his humanity precisely because of his divinity:

---

[45] *Mix.* 325–9.

As the whole of His body, stretched out upon the Cross, so the whole of His soul, His whole advertence, His whole consciousness, a mind awake, a sense acute, a living co-operation, a present, absolute intention, not a virtual permission, not a heartless submission, this did He present to His tormentors. His passion was an action; He lived most energetically, while He lay languishing, fainting, and dying. Nor did He die, except by an act of the will; for He bowed His head, in command as well as in resignation, and said, 'Father, into thy hands I commend My spirit;' He gave the word, He surrendered His soul, He did not lose it.

The last two sentences might seem to impugn the reality of Christ's humanity, but Newman is clear and emphatic that this is not the case: 'God was the sufferer; God suffered in His human nature; the sufferings belonged to God, and were drunk up, were drained out to the bottom of the chalice, because God drank them; not tasted or sipped, not flavoured, disguised by human medicaments, as man disposes of the cup of anguish.' Just as human suffering is greater than animal suffering because of human consciousness, so Christ's passion was of an extraordinary nature because of its unique psychological character—'He walks forth into a mental agony with as definite an action as if it were some bodily torture.' Christ's suffering was therefore essentially mental rather than physical. In answer to the objection that one would expect Christ to 'be supported under His trial by the consciousness of innocence and the anticipation of triumph', Newman contends that in fact 'His trial consisted in the withdrawal, as of other causes of consolation, so of that very consciousness and anticipation.' And 'as men of self-command can turn from one thought to another at their will, so much more did He deliberately deny Himself the comfort, and satiate Himself with the woe'. Having argued that Christ's psychological suffering was uniquely painful, Newman now comes to the paradoxical conclusion that the actual experience that caused such terrible anguish was the kind of experience that ordinary human beings experience with comparative indifference:

> He had to bear what is well known to us, what is familiar to us, but what to Him was woe unutterable. He had to bear that which is so easy a thing to us, so natural, so welcome, that we cannot conceive of it as of a great endurance, but which to Him had the scent and the poison of death—He had...to bear the weight of sin...He had to bear the sin of the whole world.

And Newman concludes the sermon by attributing Christ's death not to physical causes but to a broken heart: 'And then, when the appointed moment arrived, and He gave the word, as His Passion had begun with His soul, with the soul did it end. He did not die of bodily exhaustion, or of bodily pain; at His will His tormented Heart broke, and He commended His Spirit to the Father.'[46]

One particular characteristic of the Christ of the Gospels that Newman noted, as we have seen, in the sermon is his *calmness*. Thus he contrasts the attitude of Jesus as his death approached with that of his disciples and the Jews.

> *He* steadily fixed His face to endure those sufferings which were the atonement for our sins, yet without aught of mental excitement or agitation; His disciples and the Jewish multitude first protested their devotion to Him in vehement language, then, the one deserting Him, the other even clamouring for His crucifixion.

The Lord's Prayer itself, Newman suggests, is typical: 'How plain and unadorned is it! How few are the words of it! How grave and solemn the petitions! What an entire absence of tumult and feverish emotion!' Even in the Garden of Gethsemane, when he 'was in distress of mind beyond our understanding', and was praying that the cup might pass from him, 'how subdued and how concise is His petition!'[47] Of course, Newman had his reasons in his Anglican preaching for emphasizing this characteristic of Christ, as, in contradistinction to the emotionalism of Evangelicalism, he wanted to maintain that the hallmark of a mature Christian spirituality is a deep calmness: 'the highest Christian temper is free from all vehement and tumultuous feeling'. That this is so is shown by the figure of Christ himself as portrayed in the Gospels: 'When does He set us an example of passionate devotion, of enthusiastic wishes, or of intemperate words?'[48]

Christ is also seen by Newman as displaying that favourite Tractarian quality of reserve in his dealing with people. Far from seeking recognition, Jesus ordered those he encountered not to publicize his miraculous cures, 'as if what is called popularity would be a dishonour to His holy name, and the applause of men would imply their right to censure':

---

[46] *Mix.* 329, 331, 334–5, 341.   [47] *PS* i.177–8, 186.
[48] *PS* i.185, 187.

He spoke as one who knew He had great favours to confer, and had nothing to gain from those who received them. Far from urging them to accept His bounty, He showed Himself even backward to confer it, inquired into their knowledge and motives, and cautioned them against entering His service without counting the cost of it. Thus sometimes He even repelled men from Him.[49]

It was not just that Newman wanted to make the person of Christ real to his hearers; he was also well aware of the perennial tendency of every age and society to look at Jesus from the perspective of their own concerns and preoccupations: 'The world...in every age...chooses some one or other peculiarity of the Gospel as the badge of its particular fashion for the time being...'. In a modern civilized society which prides itself on its compassion and concern for human rights, there was the danger of a soft kind of Christianity, lacking in 'firmness, manliness, godly severity'. Newman thought that this deficiency led to a distortion of the virtue of charity, in so far as an 'element of zeal and holy sternness' was needed 'to temper and give character to the languid, unmeaning benevolence which we misname Christian love'.[50]

Newman's Jesus is not only the Jesus of compassion, the 'caring' Jesus, but also the Jesus who drove the money-lenders out of the temple with cords, the Jesus who inspires both fear and love, who felt affection for the rich young man but who also made the severest of demands on him. This is a Jesus who 'loves us, yet speaks harshly to us that we may learn to cherish mixed feelings towards Him. He hides Himself from us, and yet calls on us, that we may hear His voice as Samuel did, and, believing, approach Him with trembling.' For the Christian, then, Newman insists, *'fear and love must go together'*. For the God who reveals himself in Jesus is not an indulgent, avuncular kind of God:

No one can love God aright without fearing Him; though many fear Him, and yet do not love Him. Self-confident men, who do not know their own hearts, or the reasons they have for being dissatisfied with themselves, do not fear God, and they think this bold freedom is to love Him. Deliberate sinners fear but cannot love Him...No one really loves another, who does not feel a certain reverence towards him.

---

[49] *PS* i.298.   [50] *PS* ii.279–80, 286.

The real Jesus of the Gospels inspires both fear and love: 'The fear of God is the beginning of wisdom...Fear and love must go together; always fear, always love, to your dying day...Till you know what it is to fear with the terrified sailors or the Apostles, you cannot sleep with Christ at your Heavenly Father's feet.' For the more we love Christ, the more we will fear him because the more we shall feel our unworthiness. Thus, while Newman insists, 'you must always fear while you hope,'" he explains this by adding, 'Your knowledge of your sins increases with your view of God's mercy in Christ.'[51]

In his preaching Newman was anxious to remove any stereotyped ideas his congregation might have about the Christ of the Gospels. He pointed out, for example, that the popular notion that Christ was a radical reformer who ignored and swept aside traditional religious forms was hardly compatible with his 'dutiful attention to the religious system under which He was born; and that, not only so far as it was directly divine, but further, where it was the ordinance of uninspired though pious men, where it was but founded on ecclesiastical authority'. Not only did Jesus present himself for baptism by John the Baptist, but his followers 'neither abandoned the Jewish rites themselves, nor obliged any others to do so who were used to them'. But this did not mean that Jesus was conventionally, let alone respectably, religious. He was in fact, Newman observes bluntly, 'what would now be called with contempt a vagrant'. That at least was what he was essentially during his active ministry, which lasted only three years. Before that he lived in obscurity in Nazareth until he was thirty. This should present a problem to an activist kind of Christian: 'How very wonderful is all this! That He should live here, doing nothing great, so long; living here, as if for the sake of living; not preaching, or collecting disciples, or apparently in any way furthering the cause which brought Him down from heaven.'[52]

Outwardly quite unremarkable, Jesus had one unique characteristic which went unnoticed because, Newman suggests, it will always go unnoticed: 'He was in all respects a man, except that He did not sin, and this great difference the many would not detect, because none of us understands those who are much better than himself: so that Christ, the sinless of God, might be living close to us, and we not discover it.' Indeed, would *we* have recognized Christ for who he

51   *PS* i.303–4, 322–3.   52   *PS* ii.70–1; vi.45; iv.241.

was any more than his contemporaries if he had been 'our next door neighbour, or one of our family'? Would we not have thought him 'strange, eccentric, extravagant, and fanciful'? Newman presses the point home relentlessly: we too would surely have rejected him had we been the Jews:

> We say, that had we had the advantage of being with Christ, we should have had stronger motives, stronger restraints against sin. I answer, that so far from our sinful habits being reformed by the presence of Christ, the chance is, that those same habits would have hindered us from recognizing Him. We should not have known He was present; and if He had even told us who He was, we should not have believed Him. Nay, had we seen His miracles (incredible as it may seem), even they would not have made any lasting impression on us.

Indeed, the terrible fact was that the people who came closest to Jesus were the very people who rejected him most dreadfully, as Newman explains in one of the most powerful passages in his sermons:

> Could men come nearer to God than when they seized Him, struck Him, spit on Him, hurried Him along, stripped Him, stretched out His limbs upon the cross, nailed Him to it, raised it up, stood gazing on Him, jeered Him, gave Him vinegar, looked close whether He was dead, and then pierced Him with a spear? O dreadful thought, that the nearest approaches man has made to God upon earth have been in blasphemy! Whether of the two came closer to Him, St. Thomas, who was allowed to reach forth his hand and reverently touch His wounds, and St. John, who rested on His bosom, or the brutal soldiers who profaned Him limb by limb, and tortured Him nerve by nerve? His Blessed Mother, indeed, came closer still to Him: and we, if we be true believers, still closer, who have Him really, though spiritually, within us; but this is another, an inward sort of approach. Of those who approached Him externally, they came nearest, who knew nothing about it.[53]

Newman is not content with making the point that the Jews behaved no differently from the way in which people in any age would have treated Jesus. Rather, he wants to impress upon us that actually we *are* doing exactly what the Jews did. For Christ has not left this earth, but is still present albeit in a different, but similarly hidden mode:

> The Holy Ghost's coming is so really His coming, that we might as well say that He was not here in the days of His flesh, when He was visibly in

---

[53] *PS* iv.242, 245–7.

this world, as deny that He is here now, when He is here by His Divine Spirit...

Next, if He is still on earth, yet is not visible (which cannot be denied), it is plain that He keeps Himself still in the condition which He chose in the days of His flesh. I mean, He is a hidden Saviour, and may be approached (unless we are careful) without due reverence and fear...It is probable, then, that we can now commit at least as great blasphemy towards Him as the Jews did first, because we are under the dispensation of that Holy Spirit, against whom even more heinous sins *can* be committed; next, because His presence now as little witnesses of itself, or is impressive to the many, as His bodily presence formerly.

This is why sinful Christians now are in a similar situation to those in Christ's time who came closest to him externally:

So is with sinners: they would walk close to the throne of God; they would stupidly gaze at it; they would touch it; they would meddle with the holiest things; they would go on intruding and prying, not meaning any thing wrong by it, but with a sort of brute curiosity, till the avenging lightnings destroyed them;—all because they have no *senses* to guide them in the matter.

For Newman concludes, employing one of the most arresting—and horrifying—images he ever employed:

sinners have no spiritual sense; they can presage nothing; they do not know what is going to happen the next moment to them. So they go fearlessly further and further among precipices, till on a sudden they fall, or are smitten and perish. Miserable beings! And this is what sin does for immortal souls; that they should be like the cattle which are slaughtered at the shambles, yet touch and smell the very weapons which are to destroy them![54]

While lamenting the ignorance of the Gospels among the Catholics of his day, Newman insisted as a Catholic preacher that Catholicism was nothing if it was not the loving contemplation of Christ—that 'energetic, direct apprehension of an unseen Lord and Saviour' which it is the work of the Church to foster at all times among Catholics:

Age passes after age, and she varies her discipline, and she adds to her devotions, and all with the one purpose of fixing her own and their gaze more fully upon the presence of her unseen Lord. She has adoringly surveyed Him, feature by feature, and has paid a separate homage

---

[54] *PS* iv.24–9.

to Him in every one. She has made us honour His Five Wounds, His Precious Blood, and His Sacred Heart. She has bid us meditate on His infancy, and the Acts of His ministry; His agony, His scourging, and His crucifixion...

In a Catholic church Christ is really present, present in the Sacrament reserved in the tabernacle, a presence that Newman thought explained the difference between Protestant and Catholic worshippers. For whereas Protestants 'are serious at prayer time, and behave with decency... mere duty, a sense of propriety, and good behaviour, these are not the ruling principles present in the mind of our worshippers':

> Wherefore, on the contrary, those spontaneous postures of devotion? why those unstudied gestures? why those abstracted countenances? why that heedlessness of the presence of others? why that absence of the shame-facedness which is so sovereign among professors of other creeds? The spectator sees the effect; he cannot understand the cause of it. *Why* is this simple earnestness of worship? *we* have no difficulty in answering. It is because the Incarnate Saviour is present in the tabernacle... It is the visible Sign of the Son of Man...[55]

If Catholicism, if Christianity, essentially consists in the contemplation of Christ, this is also the key to its successful propagation. It is Christ who is the cause and ground of faith. In one of his Catholic sermons, 'The Secret Power of Divine Grace' (1856), Newman takes over and adapts a striking passage from one of his Anglican sermons, 'Invisible Presence of Christ' (1841). In the earlier sermon he had preached that the gospel answers a deeply felt need by filling the emptiness of the human heart:

> Man is not sufficient for his own happiness; he is not happy except the Presence of God be with him. When he was created, God breathed into him that supernatural life of the Spirit which is his true happiness; and when he fell, he lost the divine gift, and with it his happiness also. Ever since he has been unhappy; ever since he has a void within him which needs filling, and he knows not how to fill it. He scarcely realizes his own need: only his actions show that he feels it, for he is ever restless when he is not dull and insensible, seeking in one thing or another that blessing which he has lost. Multitudes, indeed, there are, whose minds have never been opened; and multitudes who stupefy and deaden their minds, till they lose their natural hunger and thirst: but, whether aware

---

[55]   *OS* 40, 42–3.

of their need or not, whether made restless by it or not, still all men have it, and the Gospel supplies it; and then, even if they did not recognize their want by nature, they at length learn it by its supply.

There is no great mystery, then, about the spread of Christianity: there was no need to look for hidden causes. The secret of its propagation is summed up in Newman's words: 'the keen, vivid, constraining glance of Christ's countenance'. It is not a philosophical or theological abstraction but 'the piercing, soul-subduing look of the Son of Man' who fulfils the otherwise unfulfillable human longing for 'an object of life'.[56] The new evangelization, Newman would insist, must preach not Christianity but Christ.

3

In the novel, the post-pagan Callista, having been successfully evangelized by Caecilius, still has to be catechized before she can become a Christian by receiving the three sacraments of initiation, baptism, confirmation, and Eucharist. The author does not tell us what instruction Caecilius's deacon Victor gives her, but from Newman's other writings we can guess the kind of thing he would have said.

First, he would have explained that the Incarnation 'establishes in the very idea of Christianity the *sacramental* principle as its characteristic'.[57] We encounter Christ not only in the Gospels and in Christian believers, but more concretely, directly, and personally in the sacraments. Like Newman, the new evangelization must explain sacraments not in terms of an impersonal quality called 'grace' but as intimate encounters with the person of Christ. By becoming man, the incarnate Word of God was able to sanctify human nature by coming 'personally' to us through the sacraments.[58] It is, as Newman put it on another occasion, 'a higher gift than grace' that 'refine[s]' our 'flesh and blood'—'God's Presence and His very Self,/And Essence all-divine'.[59] Through 'His indwelling', Christ is the 'immediate' source of 'spiritual life to each of His elect individually'.[60] Sacraments, then, are integral to Christianity not only because of the Incarnation but

---

[56]   *SD* 312–13; *OS* 52–3.   [57]   *Dev.* 325.   [58]   *Ath.* ii.193.
[59]   *VV* 364.   [60]   *Ath.* ii.193.

because Christianity is 'of a personal nature, and implies the acknowledgement of a particular Providence, of a God speaking, not merely to the world at large, but to this person or that, to one and not to another'. The Bible, on the other hand, 'is a common possession, and speaks to one man as much and as little as to his neighbour'. However, human nature 'requires something special', something of a highly personal character, such as a sacrament.[61] As Newman explains in one of the most evocative passages in his Anglican sermons, the sacraments are supremely personal, but nonetheless elusive, encounters with the incarnate Son of God, whose incarnation demands a continuing incarnational presence in the form of material signs which effect what they signify:

> In these is manifested in greater or less degree, according to the measure of each, that Incarnate Saviour, who is one day to be our Judge, and who is enabling us to bear His presence then, by imparting it to us in measure now. A thick black veil is spread between this world and the next. We mortal men range up and down it, to and fro, and see nothing. There is no access through it into the next world. In the Gospel this veil is not removed; it remains, but every now and then marvellous disclosures are made to us of what is behind it. At times we seem to catch a glimpse of a Form which we shall hereafter see face to face. We approach, and in spite of the darkness, our hands, or our head, or our brow, or our lips become, as it were, sensible of the contact of something more than earthly. We know not where we are, but we have been bathing in water, and a voice tells us that it is blood. Or we have a mark signed upon our foreheads, and it spake of Calvary. Or we recollect a hand laid upon our heads, and surely it had the print of nails in it, and resembled Him who with a touch gave sight to the blind and raised the dead. Or we have been eating and drinking; and it was not a dream surely, that One fed us from His wounded side, and renewed our nature by the heavenly meat He gave. Thus in many ways He, who is Judge to us, prepares us to be judged,—He, who is to glorify us, prepares us to be glorified, that He may not take us unawares; but that when the voice of the Archangel sounds, and we are called to meet the Bridegroom, we may be ready.[62]

Victor would not have said much to Callista about the sacrament of confirmation, which merely confirms the sacrament of baptism, but he would have had much to say about the sacraments of baptism and

---

[61] *Jfc.* 323.   [62] *PS* v.10–11.

Eucharist. He would have explained to Callista that baptism is the primary sacrament which conveys to the baptized person the Holy Spirit, through whom we become a member of the Church and in whom Christ becomes intimately present to us. For baptism 'is an instrument of the Holy Ghost' who 'dwells in the child baptized'.[63] But, as we have seen,[64] the Holy Spirit does not come to take the place of Christ but to make him present, for where the Holy Spirit is there Christ is necessarily present too 'by His Divine Spirit'. Like the Holy Spirit, Christ is 'an inward presence' because he is 'given to us by the Spirit'. There is no question of the Holy Spirit taking the place of Christ:

> Let us not for a moment suppose that God the Holy Ghost comes in such sense that God the Son remains away. No; He has not so come that Christ does not come, but rather He comes that Christ may come in His coming. Through the Holy Ghost we have communion with Father and Son…The Holy Spirit causes, faith welcomes, the indwelling of Christ in the heart. Thus the Spirit does not take the place of Christ in the soul, but secures that place to Christ.[65]

The Eucharist, Victor the deacon would have explained to Callista, completes the sacraments of initiation: when she has received Holy Communion she will have become a full Christian, having experienced 'the foretaste of heaven' in that 'invisible Presence, whom they shall hereafter see face to face'.[66] The doctrine of the Incarnation, he would have pointed out to her, demands the doctrine of the Real Presence:

> No one realizes the Mystery of the Incarnation but must feel disposed towards that of Holy Communion. Let us pray Him to give us an earnest longing after Him—a thirst for His Presence—an anxiety to find Him—a joy on hearing that He is to be found, even now, under the veil of sensible things,—and a good hope that *we* shall find Him there.[67]

Just as Caecilius had moved Callista with his eloquent and impassioned insistence that only a personal God, the God of Christianity, can satisfy the deepest human need, the sense of unfulfilment, so too Victor would surely have invoked his own joy in the Eucharist, albeit not exactly in the words of the Anglican Newman:

---

[63] *PS* iii.271, 283; viii.57.   [64] See Chapter 2, section 3, p. 56–7.
[65] *PS* iv.248–9; v.138; vi.126.   [66] *PS* vii.159.   [67] *PS* vi.151.

...how pleasant to come, day after day, quietly and calmly, to kneel before our Maker,—week after week, to meet our Lord and Saviour. How soothing will then be the remembrance of His past gifts! we shall remember how we got up early in the morning, and how all things, light or darkness, sun or air, cold or freshness, breathed of Him,—of Him, the Lord of glory, who stood over us, and came down upon us, and gave Himself to us, and poured forth milk and honey for our sustenance, though we saw Him not. Surely we have all, and abound: we are full.[68]

When she received Holy Communion for the first time, Victor might have added, she would not only be encountering Christ in the most intimate and personal way, but she would actually become Christ, for when we eat his body and drink his blood he enters into us and becomes one with us: 'We eat the sacred bread, and our bodies become sacred; they are not ours; they are Christ's; they are instinct with that flesh which saw not corruption; they are inhabited by His Spirit; they become immortal; they die but to appearance, and for a time; they spring up when their sleep is ended, and reign with Him for ever.'[69] As for Callista herself, she would have been thrilled to discover that that that 'intimate Divine Presence in the heart', which seemed to answer her deepest aspirations and needs, was present not only in the heart but also in the form of food and drink—food and drink to give her life:

> He who is at the right hand of God, manifests Himself in that Holy Sacrament as really and fully as if He were visibly there...Such is the glorious presence which faith sees in the Holy Communion, though every thing looks as usual to the natural man. Not gold or precious stones, pearls of great price or gold of Ophir, are to the eye of faith so radiant as those lowly elements which He, the Highest, is pleased to make the means of conveying to our hearts and bodies His own gracious self.[70]

Because the 'real presence' is not actually an unreal presence but the 'Divine Presence' itself, the Eucharist, Callista would have been instructed, is 'the greatest and highest of all the Sacramental mysteries':

> Christ, who died and rose again for us, is in it spiritually present, in the fullness of His death and of His resurrection. We call His presence in this Holy Sacrament a spiritual presence, not as if 'spiritual' were but a name or mode of speech, and He were really absent, but by way of

---

[68] *PS* v.283.   [69] *PS* i.275.   [70] *PS* iv.148.

expressing that He who is present there can neither be seen nor heard; that He cannot be approached or ascertained by any of the senses; that He is not present carnally, though He is really present.[71]

And so that quest for 'some object which may possess me', 'something to rest upon', 'something to love',[72] would finally have come to an end for Callista. But it would no longer be an object or a thing but a Person, the God who became human in Jesus Christ, who is still present in the souls of the baptized through the Holy Spirit, and who both possesses us and is possessed by us when we eat his body and drink his blood in the Eucharist. To adapt the words of the pope who called for a 'new evangelization', now 'Christ the Redeemer fully reveals [Callista] to [herself]', since to 'understand' herself 'thoroughly' she 'must... draw near to Christ'.[73] Now she fully understands why she felt so unfulfilled, so unhappy, 'with an over-flowing heart, with keen affections, with a yearning' for 'something to love'.[74]

---

[71] *PS* vi.136–7.   [72] See section 1, p. 135.

[73] Pope John Paul II, *Redemptoris Missio*, art. 2, quoting his encyclical *Redemptor Hominis*, art. 10.

[74] See section 1, p. 135.

Conclusion

Newman was asked repeatedly by two bishops, Bishop Félix Dupanloup of Orleans and Bishop Thomas Brown of Newport, to attend the First Vatican Council as their personal theologian, but he refused both requests on the ground that his 'vocation' did not 'lie in such ecclesiastical gatherings'.[1] Since Dupanloup was the leader of the bishops opposing the extreme Ultramontanes, there were very good reasons why he would have wished to have Newman as his theological adviser and why Newman might have seen it as his duty to accept the invitation. If, then, Newman could refuse Dupanloup, there is every reason to suppose that he would have refused similar requests had he been alive when Pope John XXIII convoked the Second Vatican Council. And, indeed, he has often been referred to as 'the absent father' at Vatican II, where his presence was certainly felt just as his absence was felt at Vatican I.

There can be no question but that Newman would have strongly supported the reformist party at Vatican II. However, reformers sooner or later invariably divide into moderate and more extreme factions, and predictably after the Council there were those who wished to interpret the texts of the conciliar documents as they stood and in the light of tradition, and, on the other hand, those who preferred to invoke what they called 'the spirit of Vatican II' and to embrace a hermeneutic of discontinuity with the past, which inevitably involved the call for a third Vatican Council that would supply whatever they deemed inadequate in the conciliar texts. The argument of this book has been that Newman would undoubtedly have aligned himself with the moderates, with the great *ressourcement* theologians such as Daniélou and De Lubac, with the young bishop Karol Wojtyla, the future Pope John Paul II, the young *peritus* Joseph Ratzinger, the future Pope Benedict XVI, and all those who wished to interpret the Council in accordance with the hermeneutic of reform in continuity.

---

[1] *LD* xxiii.396.

The theology that triumphed at Vatican II was the same kind of theology that Newman had himself gained from his own study of the sources in the scriptures and the Fathers. True, there was only one place in the conciliar documents, as we have seen, where a more or less direct reference was made to Newman. Nevertheless, Newman's writings on those subjects that occupied the Council offer a balanced, corrective commentary on the conciliar documents. Moreover, Newman's theology of Councils, a theology that lay hidden in private letters and that only began to be published eight years after the ending of the Council, contains, as we have seen, a number of salutary warnings and predictions that could have provided an illuminating, not to say consoling, commentary on events during and after the tumultuous years of the Council.

The two most important contributions that I think Newman can make to the ongoing debate about the meaning and significance of Vatican II relate to its most controversial document, *Dignitatis Humanae*, and its most important document, *Lumen Gentium*. As regards the former Declaration, I hope I have shown how illuminatingly Newman's seven 'tests' or 'notes' of doctrinal development demonstrate how what appeared to be a drastic reversal of Church teaching can in fact be reconciled with the past teaching, can be seen as certainly a change but a change in continuity with past teaching. For if the Declaration is to be seen as a theological *volte face* by the Church, then one must conclude either with the Lefebvrists that Vatican II is a heretical Council or with liberal Catholics that the Church simply does and can revoke its teachings.

As regards the Constitution on the Church, the full significance of what must surely be the most fundamental text of all the conciliar documents, the text in which a Council, almost entirely preoccupied with the Church, formulated its understanding of the essential nature of the Church, becomes much more luminous in the light of what Newman has to say about religious ideas becoming clearer in the course of time, as well as in the light of what he says about the importance of what a Council fails to say, what it is silent about. The rise of the new ecclesial movements and communities, which realize in the flesh the organic ecclesiology of the baptized that we find in those first two chapters of *Lumen Gentium*, and which are the Holy Spirit's response to the post-conciliar perceived need for a 'new evangelization', would certainly have delighted Newman, the leader of the Oxford Movement, who had hoped as Catholic that a similar movement would arise in the face of anti-Catholicism, and who had brought to England the Oratory of St Philip Neri, which, he was well aware, had begun not as the priestly congregation it had become, but as a community remarkably similar to a contemporary ecclesial community. Very conscious both as an Anglican and as a Catholic of the charismatic dimension of the Church, Newman would hardly have disagreed with the then Cardinal Ratzinger in seeing the new ecclesial movements and communities as constituting the fifth great charismatic surge in the history of the Church.

The Council's silence about evangelization would, I think, have struck Newman, who was preoccupied already in his own time with the justification of religious belief in the context of an increasingly secularized culture and society. And he would, I hope, have been gratified to see his neglected novel, *Callista*, given here at last the attention he rightly considered it deserved. For the kind of apologetic it dramatizes is surely the kind of apologetic that he would have recommended to a Church committed to a new kind of evangelization, the evangelization of secular post-Christians.

John Henry Newman was beatified by Pope Benedict XVI in 2010. In the likely event of his canonization, he will assuredly be declared a Doctor of the Church. In this book I hope to have given some reasons why in that case he is likely to be seen as the counterpart, in the Church of the Second Vatican Council, of St Robert Bellarmine, the Doctor *par excellence* of the Tridentine Church.

Index

Printed and bound by CPI Group (UK) Ltd, Croydon, CR0 4YY